Money Skills for Teen Girls

Budgeting, Investing, Money Management, and More

Essential Personal Finance Strategies for Smart Teenage Girls – Learn, Apply, and Succeed

The Mentor Bucket

Table of Contents

Introduction

*"Never spend your money before
you have earned it."*
Thomas Jefferson

Have you ever scrolled through your favorite social media feed and seen influencers living their best lives? Maybe you watch videos of them traveling, wearing the latest designers, and eating at fancy restaurants. You're sitting there wondering how they could afford all that expensive stuff at such a young age while you struggle to make your allowance stretch until the end of the month.

Perhaps you've once stood in the middle of a store, staring at something you've always wanted, but after doing the mental math of *If I buy this now, how do I survive the next few months?* you immediately shut down the idea of getting it. Those inner debates you have with yourself when you see something you like usually stem from a lack of mastering your money game. Luckily, you're reading this book, so that problem is about to be solved.

We've all been there—those moments when we're torn between treating ourselves to something awesome and still needing to be smart about our cash. But who says you can't have that beautiful dress and still have money in your savings? The idea is to strike a balance, and that's what we'll discuss in this book.

Over the years, I've realized that understanding how to manage money isn't about saying "no" to everything you love. It's all about taking charge of your financial future in ways that set you up for success. When you find the sweet spot, you can enjoy buying the things you love while still being smart about it.

So, whether it's earning your own cash from a side gig or part-time job, budgeting well, or investing in the right places, it's important that you learn to navigate the world of money. I get it; personal finance can feel huge and overwhelming, especially since it involves confusing terms and numbers. Well, that's part of my motivation for writing this book.

In this book, I will guide you through all the ins and outs of money management in ways that are fun, practical, and easy to understand. I'll teach you how to take control of your finances like a boss lady and make smart decisions that set you up for success, now and in the future.

Though you might have often felt confused or overwhelmed when it comes to money matters, by reading this book, you're already saying goodbye to such uncertainties. It will boost your confidence about finances and serve as your roadmap to financial independence. You'll learn how to budget, save, invest, and make great financial decisions. It is fully packed with practical tips and strategies to help you tackle any financial challenge that comes your way.

So, what do I aim to solve by writing this book? Well, when it comes to personal finance, there's often a lack of resources tailored specifically to the needs and interests of teen girls. I write this book because I believe in financial education and how it can transform the lives of young women. I aim to arm teen girls with the skills and knowledge needed to dream big, take risks, and build the future they deserve; I hope you get empowered to do this.

I believe that understanding money isn't just about numbers, but it entails unlocking a world of many possibilities and opportunities. As a teen girl, you're navigating new experiences and challenges daily, so it's best to equip yourself with the right tools to prepare you for adulthood.

Whether you want to travel around the world, start your own business, have robust savings, or build a solid financial foundation, this book will support you every step of the way. Use it as your secret tool to unlock a future where you'll be calling the shots, just as many amazing women are doing today.

Among them is Mikaila Ulmer, who started *Me & the Bees Lemonade* at the age of 4, using her grandma's recipe and local honey. With consistency and determination, she got her lemonade stocked in big-name stores like Whole Foods and Target. She is a good example of starting young and slaying the game!

Bella Weems is another great example. As a teen girl, she started *Origami Owl* at the age of 14. Who would've believed that selling customizable lockets at house parties could blow up to hit over $250 million in revenue by the time she turned 18? Well, she made it happen.

And there's Isabella Rose Taylor, who launched her own fashion brand at the age of 13. By the time she was 16, her designs were already being sold at Nordstrom. Do you know who else slammed it even before her teenage years? Gabrielle Jordan Williams! She started her business at the age of 9. At such a young age, she not only became a bestselling author but also a motivational speaker and founder of a mentoring institute for young entrepreneurs.

Finally, we have Madison Robinson, who came up with the idea for *FishFlops* at the age of 8. Her colorful flip-flops caught the attention of many notable people, including Oprah Winfrey and Ellen DeGeneres, and the business grew to be worth millions.

If you look at these girls, you'd think they were born to be bosses. Well, they learned to be shining examples of what is possible when one is passionate, prepared, and ready to take the initiative. Their lives serve as an inspiration for other teen girls everywhere, proving to us that age shouldn't be a barrier to success. Just as they did, you can take charge of your financial future with confidence and clarity.

So, here's to you, the next generation of independent female leaders! I am confident that you can shatter stereotypes, break down barriers, and show the world what you're capable of.

Ready to get started? Let's go!

CHAPTER 1
The Basics of Money

Money, money, money—you've definitely heard the rustle of bills exchanging hands and the sounds of coins jingling together. While some say money is a universal language, others say it makes the world go around. But have you ever paused to think of what this enigmatic force means to you?

In a world where most decisions you make circle back to money, it's important to understand the influence and power it has. Money is the fuel driving economies and the force that makes things happen. It is more than just a means of exchange, as it dictates your life choices and shapes your destiny. Wondering how? This chapter will shed more light on that.

Let's say you've been eyeing this cool thing you've wanted for ages. You've saved up your allowance for weeks, and now you're standing in the store ready to buy it. But then, as you're about to hand over your cash, you start to wonder if you're making the right decision. You're also thinking about that girl's night out you don't want to miss.

Sound familiar? Of course. We've all been there—those moments when we're confused about the right financial decision to make. Regardless of how overwhelmed we may feel about money decisions, we need to know that understanding the basics of money isn't just about making tough decisions but also setting yourself up for success. It's about having the right skills to keep you informed and updated on your finances and the decisions that will shape your future.

To set the foundation, this chapter will discuss what money is, how it works, the importance of financial literacy, and simple money management skills every teen girl should know. So, whether you're new to personal finance or you already have your toe in it, this chapter aims to change how you think about money.

Understanding Money

Money is a tool for trading goods and services; it's the universal language of transactions since you give someone money in exchange for something you need or want.

Anything that's generally acceptable as payment for goods, services, and debt satisfaction in a country or socio-economic context can be referred to as money. Money isn't just cold hard cash. It comes in different forms and shapes, ranging from coins and bills to even digital currency such as online payments and credit cards. If you've ever tapped your phone to pay for a snack or buy something online, you've just used money without physically touching it.

So, how does money work?

Before money was invented, there were other means people used to carry out transactions. Specifically, people relied on bartering to trade the goods they had for the ones they needed. However, this caused the issue of a double coincidence of wants. That is, the transactions can only happen if both parties have something that the other needs. However, with the invention of money, this issue was eliminated by having money act as an intermediary good.

As economies became even more complex, money had to be standardized into currencies. This reduced the cost of transactions by easing, measuring, and comparing value. The representation of money became abstract, from stamped coins and precious metals to paper notes. And in this modern era, we have electronic records.

The Value for Money

Have you ever heard the quote, "*Nothing is free even in a free town?*" Money is the reason that quotes exist. Although money is not the only thing that can be used in human exchanges, it is the most common thing people accept. The basic value of money is as a unit used to purchase items or pay for services, but there is more to money than earning it and paying for things.

One important feature of money is that it isn't just about buying things but also about earning them. For example, whether you're babysitting for your neighbors, doing chores at home, or working a part-time job, every penny you earn represents your time and effort. You are trading a piece of yourself for a paper that has worth.

A one-dollar bill can be just a piece of paper, but it represents something bigger—value! This value makes it possible to trade a one-dollar bill for a candy bar. Money has that power!

As mentioned earlier, money needs to have value for it to be useful. Otherwise, it is just a worthless number or piece of paper. Several countries have currencies that can't pay for much because that money has lost its value. The money in your account or your hand can lose its value in the same way. What can contribute to the value of money?

The way humans spend money can go a long way toward improving or reducing the value of money. Money itself is worth something on its own. If you think I'm wrong, take out a $20 bill and calculate all the things you can buy with that paper. You will find out what $20 means to you. If you give that same amount to another person, it would mean something else. Some people might consider the $20 that would buy one week's worth of snacks for you as next to nothing. Money has value, and that value is why it is acceptable as an item to be used for exchanges.

As a symbol, money can be given to someone for the purchase of an item or for payment of services. In the same way, you can request money from another person when you've babysat for them or sold them cookies. Whether you care to admit it or not, it would be hard to survive in the world without money, which is why it's crucial to understand the value of money.

The value of money can become unstable if the country's market pricing is too high or too low, otherwise known as inflation and deflation. That situation can work for better or for worse, but where money is involved, it is always better to stand in the middle. With a proper understanding of the value of money, you will know how to spend wisely, save, and invest properly.

While considering the value of money in your life, you must consider the money you have available to you. The funds you have now have more value than the ones you expect to have later on. A basic example is that you can't go to a mall without money in your account and tell the store to give you the latest iPhone and expect a payment in three months.

The staff at the counter will expect upfront payment for the item you want to purchase. Some may ask for a percentage of the price depending on their payment policies. Imagine how embarrassed you would be when you told them you didn't have the money to pay. You can spend only what you have presently, so spending money that hasn't gone into your account yet will either be impossible or leave you in debt.

Money can be valuable to you as an exchange medium, but it can also be used to save in your account. That alone brings future value that you don't know about yet. Another value for money is that it can be a way to evaluate how much your wealth is.

The Importance of Financial Literacy

You might have heard about financial literacy before, but what does it mean? Financial literacy isn't just a buzzword, it's a critical money skill every teen girl should learn to empower them in making informed financial decisions.

Let's think of financial literacy as your secret weapon for navigating the world of money like a pro. It helps you learn and understand how money works and how to make smart decisions with your finances. I tell you, it's a game-changer.

So, let's talk about the importance of financial literacy.

- **It makes you feel empowered**

Knowing how money works puts you in control of your expenditures and income. When you're financially well-informed, you're not just following along mindlessly; rather, you're making thoughtful financial choices that affect your life. When you learn to budget your allowance, save for a major purchase, and make future plans, you take control of your financial future, which allows you to shape and transform your life.

- **It's there for you to gain independence**

At one point in your life, you need to be independent and all by yourself make decisions that affect you. Imagine graduating from high school and heading for college or setting out on your first job. Financial literacy in subjects such as managing your finances, taking out a loan, and paying your bills prepares you for the big decisions when you're faced with them. Financial literacy prepares you to meet these challenges with confidence, paving the road for a more self-sufficient future.

- ## It offers security

Let's be honest—life can be unpredictable, from hazards such as unforeseen bills to economic recessions. Remember how people lost their means of livelihood during the COVID-19 pandemic? Having a good understanding of financial fundamentals can help you prepare for and weather such storms. Whether it's creating an emergency fund or understanding the value of insurance, financial literacy serves as a safety net in an uncertain environment.

- ## It gives better opportunities

Money is like a master key that opens doors, simple and plain. Whether you're planning to start a new business, pursue higher education, or travel the world, financial literacy empowers you with the right tools to unlock a world of opportunities. It's like a master key to your dreams, allowing you to pursue whatever ignites your soul.

- ## It unlocks financial freedom

Remember that financial literacy is about ending the cycle of poverty and inequality, not just about you. Learning skills and gaining knowledge to build a financial future will change your life and that of future generations.

Easy Money Management Skills Every Teen Girl Should Know

Let's discuss two hands-on money management techniques that will help you succeed: creating a bank account and keeping tabs on your spending. Although it may seem a little tasking or boring, knowing these fundamentals can drastically improve the way you manage your finances.

1. Opening a Bank Account

To start with, let's discuss opening a bank account. Consider a bank account as your headquarters for finances—it's where you store your money, ensure its security, and even help it expand. It's also far safer than hiding cash beneath your mattress. (Really, don't do that.)

Contrary to popular belief, opening a bank account is simple. Let's examine each phase of the procedure in more detail.

- **Research**: Begin by looking up several banks online or in your community. Consider the kinds of accounts they provide, the costs associated with them, the required minimum balance, and any unique features or benefits they offer. Think about things such as the bank's standing, available customer support, and branch and atm accessibility.

- **Choose a Bank**: Select a bank that best suits your needs and tastes after doing your study. Think about things such as the bank's address, operating hours, online banking capabilities, and any exclusive deals or bonuses they might provide when you open an account with them.

- **Gather Required Documents**: Make sure you have all the required documents with you before you visit the bank. Usually, this comprises:
  - **Identity proof:** Bring a photo ID from the government such as a passport, driver's license, or state ID.

  - **Social Security number:** To open some kinds of accounts and to file taxes, you'll need to supply your SSN.

  - **Proof of address:** Utility bills, lease agreements, or mail delivered to your current address are examples of the kinds of documents that some banks may need.

  In addition to documentation, if you're under the age of 18, you might need a parent or legal guardian to go with you to the bank and co-sign the account.

- **Visit the Bank**: Go to the preferred bank branch during business hours. You can schedule an appointment to avoid long waits.

- **Speak with a Bank Representative**: As soon as you arrive at the bank, inform the bank's receptionist that you would like to open an account. They'll put you in touch with a bank agent who can help you with the procedure.

- **Choose an Account Type**: Based on your requirements and financial objectives, the bank professional will assist you in selecting the best kind of account. A savings account, certificate of deposit (CD), money market account, or basic checking account could all fall under this category. Think about things such as costs, interest rates, account features, and accessibility of your funds.

- **Fill Out an Application**: After selecting an account type, you must complete an application. Your personal information, such as name, address, date of birth, SSN, and, if relevant, work details, will be requested on this form. Before applying, make sure to double-check and verify the accuracy of all the information.

- **Make an Initial Deposit**: An initial deposit may be needed to open an account with some banks. Depending on the account type you intend to open, the deposit amount could be as low as $25 or higher than that. This deposit can typically be made using cash, a money order, a cheque, or a transfer from another account.

- **Receive Your Account Materials**: The bank representative will provide you with your account documents when you've finished the application and made your first deposit. This usually consists of a welcome packet with crucial account information, a debit card (if applicable), and any other pertinent disclosures or paperwork.

- **Set Up Online Banking (Optional)**: If your bank offers online banking services, your account officer or the bank representative may help you set up your online account access. With your online banking app, you can effortlessly manage your account—checking your balance, tracking transactions, transferring money, and carrying out other banking services using your mobile phone or computer.

- **Review Account Terms and Fees**: Remember to review the fees and terms associated with your new account. Before leaving the bank, take some time to review all the terms and fees that are linked with your new account. Details such as monthly maintenance costs, minimum balance requirements, overdraft fees, atm fees, and other such charges should be carefully reviewed. Make sure you understand the potential implications of these fees for your account as well as how to avoid them.

- **Sign Necessary Documents**: Sign all the required paperwork to complete the account-opening procedure. These could contain disclosures, account agreements, signature cards, and any other documentation the bank requires. For your records, make sure you maintain copies of all documents.

If you're able to complete these steps, then congratulations— you've successfully opened your bank account. Don't be shy; take a moment to celebrate reaching this significant turning point on your financial journey.

2. Tracking Your Expenses

Keeping records and tracking your spending is essential to good financial management. It helps you make wise decisions and keep track of your financial objectives by providing you with a financial roadmap that shows you just where your money is going. Here is a more detailed look at how to keep track of your expenses:

- **Select a Tracking Method**: There are several ways to keep tabs on your spending, so pick the one that suits you the best.

    i.   **Pen and Paper:** List all of your expenses in a tangible notepad or journal.

    ii. **Spreadsheet:** Create a budget spreadsheet where you may enter your spending using an application such as Google Sheets or Excel.

    iii. **Mobile Apps:** You can track spending on the move, classify transactions, and create reports with the many budgeting apps that are available.

- **Record Every Expense**: Develop the habit of keeping a note of every expense, regardless of size. This covers purchases made with checks, cash, credit cards, or any other form of payment. Keep accurate and thorough records of all of your spending as soon as it happens.

- **Categorize Your Expenses**: To make tracking and analysis of your costs easier, categorize your spending. Some of the common categories include:

    i.   Accommodation (lease or mortgage, utilities, and insurance)

    ii. Transportation (fuel, public transportation, auto repair)

    iii. Food (eating out, groceries)

    iv. Entertainment (films, live performances, subscriptions)

    v.   Personal (grooming, attire, and presents)

    vi. Debt (loans, payments on credit cards)

    vii. Savings (contributions to savings accounts or retirement funds)

- **Set Budget Limits**: Considering your income and financial objectives, decide how much you wish to spend in each area of your expenses. Establish reasonable spending caps for every category and make every effort to adhere to them.

- **Track Frequently**: Establish the practice of tracking your costs on a daily or monthly basis. This can assist you in managing your money and locating any areas where you could be overspending.

- **Examine and Evaluate**: Examine your spending logs regularly to make sure that your expenditures are in line with your financial objectives and budget. Examine trends, patterns, and places where you might improve your financial circumstances by making changes.

- **Make Adjustments**: Depending on your findings, make any required changes to your spending habits or budget. This could include cutting back on wasteful costs, finding ways to save money, or reallocating funds to various areas.

- **Stay Consistent**: When keeping track of spending, consistency is essential. To enjoy the advantages of improved financial awareness and control, include it in your daily practice and maintain it over time.

Tracking your expenses meticulously and consistently will provide useful insights into your spending habits, allowing you to make more informed financial decisions. It's a simple yet effective tool for achieving your financial objectives and creating a more secure future.

In addition to creating a bank account and tracking costs, we'll review a few additional basic money management techniques later in this book. They are budgeting, saving, dealing with interest and debt, paying taxes, and investing.

Teens who master these easy money management skills will have a solid basis for financial success and independence as they enter adulthood. These abilities not only assist teens in making sound financial decisions in the short term, but they also lay the framework for long-term wealth creation and achievement.

That's it for the first chapter. Stay with me as we discuss budgeting in the next chapter.

CHAPTER 2
Budgeting Like a Boss

No one has their entire life figured out; even those in their early 30s are still trying to figure things out. I believe you must have come across some people who look like they have figured things out; they seem to earn as much as you do but are living a more financially stable lifestyle than you. They show that they are real bosses of their game; they always dress well, seem to have everything going smoothly for them, and have significant savings for emergencies.

While others struggle to stretch their allowance till the end of the month, there's always that one classmate who can afford to buy nice things for themselves without stressing. If this is the lifestyle you aim for, then you have to put in the effort; not just to make the money but also to manage it. When you see these people, you may admire them, but do you know that this can be you, too? Their secret is simple—budgeting. And that's what we'll be discussing in this chapter.

Budgeting doesn't mean spending less or not spending at all. It means getting ready to challenge yourself to live off a certain amount for a particular period. Just as high schools will designate a budget for clubs to host their projects, life can work that way, too. Whatever you want to do should be within a budget.

Let's start by discussing what budgeting entails and why you should get on board with it.

Budgeting and Why It Matters

Budgeting is simply a plan but with money. It involves planning for everything you need to survive, including the things you do for pleasure. The goal in budgeting is to discipline yourself and your spending habits; to spend less and save more. Sticking to a budget helps you get accountable for yourself.

Living life on a budget is in no way a disadvantage. It may seem constricting at first, but you'll feel immense pride for sticking with it in the long run. In your late teens and launching into your twenties may not seem like a decisive time in your life financially. So, a lot of young girls make the mistake of assuming they don't need to know about personal finance until they're older. The truth is, if you don't learn now, you may never know how to manage your money when you are older. In the worst case, teen girls procrastinate until they're 26, living with debts because they never learned how to live on a budget.

Budgeting is something you have to stick with if you want good results. If anything, it gives you an edge over others because you have more control over your financial life. The process of making the budget itself helps you learn about yourself. When you think, *"I'm not earning enough to be on a budget,"* or *"Budgeting isn't for everyone,"* imagine how much money you will save if you try living on a budget for one month. You might be surprised by your own discipline.

When you survive living on a budget for a month without cheating yourself, the thrill you feel is amazing. After living through the first few months, you will find out that you have more trust in yourself. You automatically check everything you buy and take note of that even without having to force yourself.

The question, *"Do I really need that new dress or pair of shoes?"* remains in your mind every time you mindlessly scroll through your phone and get tempted. With discipline comes improved accountability. Without having to look at your bank statement, you will know where your money goes and find it easy to check for irregularities.

There are many advantages to living on a budget. Your lifestyle is bound to be so much better when you live within a budget because you are planning for everything. A budget helps you plan for the clothes you wear, the food you eat, the places you go to with friends, the concerts you attend, and even the games you can afford. Instead of wondering where the money is going to come from, you can budget based on your current income.

Budgeting also helps with paying back debts. If you have

taken out a loan or have credit debt to pay off, living on a budget might be a way out for you. The fastest way to pay debt is by earning the payments, but if you put all of your earnings into paying your debt, you will have nothing to survive on. You can start by putting yourself on a budget of a percentage of your income while the rest goes toward paying that debt.

The budget you have created will help you know how long your food items, toiletries, etc. will last before they need to be paid for again. With that in mind, you can segment how much of your income goes into paying the debt. If you have no debt to pay, then budgeting can be more enjoyable for you because you will get more reward for your discipline.

This lifestyle has a lot of room for saving. If you're surviving on half your income, the other half can go into savings to purchase assets, go on a vacation, or do whatever you wish to do with the funds later. Budgeting makes saving easy since you only have to think of the things in the budget and not what you have left. Your savings can, in turn, be very helpful in emergencies that you can't control.

The best thing about living on a budget is that you can stop yourself from overspending. With a budget, everything is accounted for, so you won't have to buy more than you need. One can easily reach their saving goal if they don't spend impulsively.

Creating Your First Budget

After deciding to live under a budget, you have to create one you can live with. It has to be something you can commit to with little room for cheating. Remember that sticking to a budget requires discipline. Even if you end up with more income one month, you either wait for next month's budget and expand it or put it off for later. Spending because you got a surprise bonus will only increase the urge to spend impulsively.

To create a budget, you have to decide on an amount you want to stick to and then put together a list of necessities for the month and how much they cost. After calculating food, water, transportation, electricity, and other necessities, you can cut costs on unnecessary things. Budgeting helps you prioritize needs and not wants.

Here is a step-by-step guide to budgeting.

Step One: Calculate your total income

The only way you can create a budget is by first knowing how much you earn. This may be a lot harder to figure out if you have multiple streams of income. First, calculate the total amount of your disposable income.

Note that whatever figure you get should not include taxes. You should remove your taxes before budgeting. When you see how much you earn in a month, you can proceed to the next step.

Step Two: Set a goal

Ensure your goal is realistic so you do not need to break your budget. Let's say you found out you spent $2,000 in a month, and you want to reduce it to $1,000 for the next year. To encourage yourself, you expect that at the end of the year, you will have saved $12,000. You can plan a reward for yourself as a way to motivate your discipline.

Step Three: Find out your spending pattern

To find this, you can use your bank statement or receipts you gathered for the month. After putting them together, filter what counts as a daily necessity and separate them from other expenditures.

Daily necessities include money you need to survive, such as for paying rent, food, water, health care, electricity, subscriptions, and transportation. Decide what is really necessary. For example, you don't need to sign up for everything for your entertainment. You may be subscribed to Spotify, Apple Music, YouTube Music, Netflix, Amazon Prime, Disney Plus, Hulu, and HBO Max. There is no way you are using all of these at once, so choose platforms that you frequent and scrap the rest to save cost.

Step Four: Write down how much your needs cost

After writing your necessities down, add them up and make sure that they fit the budget with a little left to spare. It is important to make your budget a little bit flexible because no one can see through every single expenditure in a month.

The goal is to reduce overspending to save money or pay debts. Whatever is left after calculating the necessities is the casual cash for anything else you might need that you don't know about yet.

Step Five: Adjust your spending pattern to fit your budget

This might be the hardest step in budgeting. Before deciding to live on a budget, you've already been used to a certain lifestyle. That is a life you no longer want to live, so you'll likely face challenges when budgeting.

There will be times when you doubt your wants are not restricted by the budget or when your craving tries to get the better of you. Remember that discipline is a very important factor in this process. Instead of wanting things you shouldn't have, adjust your lifestyle to suit your budget.

Tips for Sticking to Your Budget

Many people find it difficult to stick to the budget that they created for themselves because it requires a completely new lifestyle, and it can be very difficult to adjust to this. It's even worse when you know that you can afford something but you are denying yourself because you want to stick to a budget.

There's also the fact that some people around you might think you're silly for choosing to live within a budget, and they might not understand why you decided to take on this self-disciplined journey. As time goes on, you may begin to wonder if you're missing out on the things that matter in life, but as a young person, you have time to experience those. If you can continue your budgeting journey, the money that you save will bring you more happiness and excitement than you can imagine.

Here are some tips that you can use to stick to your budget.

- **Understand the need to budget**

First of all, you must not forget why you wanted to go on a budget in the first place. It might be to save money, to buy an asset, or to pay up debt. If you give up your budgeting journey halfway, you may not achieve the goal.

As stated earlier in this chapter, let's say you're trying to cut $1000 in a former $2000 lifestyle for a year. You expect that at the end of the year, you're going to have $12,000 in your savings, but if you don't stick to the budget, you're going to end up with way less.

- **Stop impulse buys**

Buying things on impulse should be a big "no" now. Impulsive buying is what necessitated the budgeting phase in the first place, so why should you go back to that? Before you make a purchase, especially when it's not part of the daily necessities that you wrote down in your budget, you need to ask yourself, *"Do I really need this?" "Can I do without this?" "For what reason do I need it?"* Your answer should determine whether you should get it or not.

- **Use emergency reserves for emergencies alone**

The spare change in the budget for emergencies should be used strictly for emergencies because you really can't predict your spending for an entire month. If at the end of the month you don't need to buy anything other than what was listed in the budget, keep the money—you don't need to spend it.

That spare change is not an opportunity for you to use the money carelessly. If you say you are going to add it to next month's budget, you will only expand the budget. Don't give yourself the freedom to buy things you don't need. Any spare change should go to your savings to avoid spilling into another wave of impulsive spending.

- **Stop counting the days**

The budgeting journey may be traveled one day at a time, but you shouldn't get too obsessed with crossing off each day. When you obsess on one day at a time, you find yourself worrying too much about how much money you are spending. Try your best to ease into the routine and not make it look like you're putting in an effort every single day. It should be a habit, and then become a lifestyle. Remember, the budget is something you want to do to help yourself. Yes, it's not compulsory, but an act of discipline you can use to hold yourself accountable for your finances.

- **Decrease the credit card limit**

Lowering your credit card limit can go a long way to helping you stick to your budget, even when your earnings qualify you for a higher limit. A lower limit can help you manage money more than you realize. To cut down on $1000 from the previous $2000 expenditure, you will reduce your credit card limit to $1000, which is your goal.

Now, anything you want to buy that exceeds the $1000 budget will not go through. While decreasing credit card limits, ensure you can pay for the important things first, such as rent, water, electricity, etc.

- **Plan meals**

Believe it or not, healthy home-cooked meals are a lot cheaper than junk food. Planning the meals you will have in a day can help you stay on budget.

For example, if you want to spend $100-$200 a week on food items, you can create a schedule of what you will eat that week. Then, go to the store and purchase those items based on your budget. You have your meals planned out weekly for the entire month, so you won't have to make careless purchases when buying food outside your home.

If you are working and it's mandatory for employees to eat out together, you either make your lunch to take to work or budget for eating out with your colleagues. Ensure that eating out won't affect the money in your budget.

Tools and Apps for Budgeting

The old-fashioned way of budgeting would be to buy a journal. However, the journal can get filled up, and you'll have to buy another one; so it continues, leading to impulsive spending. However, thanks to advancements in technology, you can now have applications on your phone that you can use to budget.

If you prefer to do your budget by hand, then it's better to go with the journal option. Journaling not only helps you keep track of your budgeting journey, but it can also track your progress.

Many apps can help you in budgeting. Regardless of the one you decide to use, ensure it can help you achieve your goals without distractions.

Here are a few budgeting apps you can try.

- **Goodbudget**

This particular app is not connected to your bank app, but it allows you to portion out your income into certain categories. These categories are referred to as envelopes. You can have an envelope each for electricity, water, food, and rent. When you have the funds that you want to budget, you assign these funds into the respective envelopes to manage them.

- **Pocketguard**

Unlike the previous application, this one is connected to your bank account. It doesn't just help you budget but also lets you see all of your finances in one place. This will, in turn, let you know how much money you have left to spend. It is not very helpful for saving money, but it is helpful for those who are trying to pay off debt through budgeting.

- **Honeydue**

If you're the kind that needs encouragement or support when budgeting or saving for anything, this particular app is for you. The Honeydue app allows you to budget with a partner. If you have a friend you plan to live with or travel with, and you both want to budget and save money for it, you should try out this application. Budgeting and saving with a partner helps you commit and be accountable.

And that's it for budgeting! Remember, you need to budget to achieve financial success. So, be flexible and mindful, and keep your eyes on the goal. Next, we'll be discussing an essential financial skill every teen girl should have—savings!

CHAPTER 3
Savings Strategies for Success

Have you ever had a piggy bank or a wooden box where you store money to be used later? Some kids were diligent enough to keep theirs for months and even years without breaking into it, but some broke it at any chance they got. Try to think back to your childhood and remember what happened to your piggy bank if you had one. It may tell you something about the past version of yourself.

The piggy bank or saving box was your parents' attempt at teaching you to save money. However, the story changes as you grow older. It will be a lot more tempting to spend money instead of saving it, especially now that you have more wants and needs.

For starters, your late teens and early twenties might be your first introduction to a large amount of money as opposed to the allowance you received as a kid. That will open your eyes to a world of things you never thought you could have. Having more money is a flex, especially if you worked hard for it, but it doesn't mean you should spend all of it. Just because you can afford it doesn't mean you should get it. As a teen girl, saving money is a skill that you must hone. With saving, you can be prepared for the surprising factors of life.

In the first chapter, we discussed money, its value, and its various forms. Now, this chapter will be focusing on saving money for financial success. Let's start by discussing the need to save money and how to go about it.

Why, How, and Where to Save

If you had one growing up, can you remember why you broke your piggy bank? Was it an emergency, or were you impatient and wanted to spend the money? If you were impatient, do you regret spending the money on the things you spent it on?

At some point in your adult life, you may wonder why no one told you adulthood would be tough. You would wonder why you were so quick to spend your savings. The good news is you are already getting yourself prepared for your teenage years by reading this book.

The most important reason to consider saving is for long-term security. While planning and budgeting are essential financial skills, no amount of budget can save you from emergencies. However, when you have savings, you won't have to worry too much about emergency expenses that may arise.

This feeling can put you in a state of financial security for quite a time as long as you are constantly putting aside some money every time you get paid. Even when living paycheck to paycheck, if you had savings, you would be fine because your savings would take care of the things your check can't.

Aside from stability, having money saved might be your gateway to financial independence from your family or support system. When you have savings, you don't need to ask your parents for money every time you need to buy something.

Saving helps you plan your expenses better, and it's not difficult to start. If you spend all the money that comes your way in the form of an allowance or money from your part-time job, you will have nothing to use to get the things you need.

The first step in starting your saving journey is deciding on a goal. This goal doesn't necessarily mean the amount you need to save; it is more about how much money you want to save every day. Let's say you have an allowance of $50 every day, and you want to start saving a part of that money. It is obvious your parents gave you that money to spend, but you want to start saving.

To decide how much to save from your allowance, you need to ask yourself, "*How much can I comfortably sacrifice from this money?*" Let's say that figure amounts to $20. You can then limit yourself to spending $30 a day and saving the remaining $20.

Now that you have decided on how much money to save,

the most important question comes into the game—where you can save money.

Before you decide on where to save your money, you have to decide in what form you want to save. It could be in cash or at the bank. If you chose the cash option, then you may want to try the piggy bank and saving box tool. When you check at a store, you can find a piggy bank or savings box of your choice. For fun, pick one that matches your personal aesthetic.

While searching for the tool, ensure that it can't break easily with minor accidents. When you start saving and you see how much you have saved, it may be tempting to spend a little bit of it when it's not necessary. This is why it is advisable to keep your money out of sight. If you keep the money in a purse or inside a booklet, you may be tempted to calculate it after adding every $20 deposit, and then you might spend it.

Aside from saving with cash or money at the bank, you can use some apps to help you save. These apps serve as phone piggy banks, and they can have really strict regulations to encourage you to take your savings seriously. Some of these apps include Pocket Guard, Acorns, and Qapital.

If you decide to go with the bank savings option, it is better to open a savings account. This is an account you shouldn't use casually but dedicate strictly to saving. All you have to do is consistently pay in or transfer the $20 every day. This might be the best option if you receive your allowance in digital currency.

Setting Up Your First Savings Account

Saving money is a step-by-step process that shouldn't be rushed. Be sure of your goals and be consistent in achieving them. If you choose to save your money at the bank, then you have to create a savings account. You can choose to save money in the account you use for your daily expenditures. However, if you want to stay motivated and avoid spending money, then it's better to create a separate account for it.

How to Set Up Your First Savings Account

Whether you're planning for your future, need to make a big purchase, or want a backup fund for emergencies, a savings account can help you reach your goals. So, how do you go about it?

Setting up your first savings account is quite similar to the process used to open a bank account.

- **Do your research**: Before you open a savings account, research different banks and credit unions to find the right fit for you. Consider factors like interest rates, fees, minimum balance requirements, and online banking options. Look for a savings account specifically designed for teens or young adults, which may offer perks such as minimum balance requirements or no monthly fees.

- **Create a plan**: Now that you know the rates, minimum balance requirements, and all the peculiarities of the account type, map out a savings plan along with strategies you'd adopt to keep to it. This can be a daily or weekly saving plan. Once you've done this, you can move on to the next step.

- **Get the required documents and create your savings account**: Before you head to the bank to open your account, don't forget to bring all the important stuff with you. You'll likely need a photo ID such as your driver's license, passport, or state ID to prove who you are. Have your Social Security number for tax stuff and some types of accounts and proof of where you live, such as a utility bill or lease agreement. If you're not yet 18, you might need a parent or guardian to tag along and help out.

When you get to the bank, tell the front desk that you're keen on setting up a savings account. They'll hook you up with someone who can walk you through the process. That person will help you pick the right savings account that fits your needs and money goals. Once you've made your choice, you'll fill out an application form with your personal information.

Some banks might ask for a little money upfront to open your account, depending on the type you're going for. After you've done all that, the bank person will hand over your account materials—a starter kit and any other necessary papers.

If you want online banking, they can help you set that up for easy access to your account anytime. Before you leave, take a quick look over the account terms and fees. Check out the interest rates, any fees, and rules on keeping a balance.

Finally, it's time to start saving! Set goals, automate transfers, and keep track of your progress. With a bit of dedication, you'll be well on your way to reaching your money goals!

Remember that the goal is to save money and avoid spending it until the deadline you have given yourself comes along. When choosing a bank, you can use the same bank you currently have an account with or a different one if you find their services better. Some banks charge a maintenance fee at a rate that can be higher than other banks.

It would be better to choose the bank with the lowest maintenance rate possible so that they don't deduct as much of your savings in the name of maintenance fees. You can find this out by reading the terms of service document the bank will provide. Before heading to the bank, you can check their website for their information so you don't have to visit multiple banks.

In some cases, the bank will allow you to open a savings account online if you already have an account with them, so that is an option you might want to explore. Even after getting the information online, it is better to read the terms of service when offered so you don't miss anything.

Helpful Saving Tips and Tricks

Saving money might be scary for you, especially when you've never succeeded in doing it. It can be an on-and-off journey, but the most important thing is your resolve to change. The minute you decide to start cutting down your expenses and saving money, you start getting tempted by things.

Sometimes, it's something as basic as getting chocolate every day, even when you don't need it. Or a new dress that is just going to join your collection of never-worn clothes. We both know you won't wear it for another six months. It could also be in buying books you won't read in the coming year.

To assist you in your saving journey, here are some tips you can use to stay consistent:

- **No debit or credit card should be available for use**

Your savings account works just as well as every other account type. You can put money in it and remove it whenever you want. To avoid spending the money that you are saving until the timeframe you set for yourself, it's better if you don't have a card.

I'm sure you realize by now how tempting it is to swipe your card at every possible impulsive purchase. This is exactly the kind of thing we're trying to avoid. You must not give room for carelessness. If you allow a debit card to be issued to you, you may accidentally use it to pay for something, eventually breaking your resolve. This is not to restrict your account but to make it difficult for you to access the funds in that account.

- **Create a budget and stick to the budget**

I know we talked about this in the previous chapter, but we need to emphasize how important it is to create a budget and stick to it.

The moment you cut down on your expenses to save, you have a smaller percentage of your income available to you. Without a budget, you may not be able to manage your savings, and you will find yourself relying on it a lot more than you should.

- **Set aside a small fund for immediate emergencies**

I know the money you are saving is for an emergency or something else, but if you keep running to your savings over the slightest discomfort, it defeats the whole point. So, it's best to set aside a small amount of money you can use for immediate emergencies.

- **Consider investment options**

Sometimes, when the money you have is easily available

in the form of cash or money in your account, you may be very tempted to use it. However, if the funds have been converted to small assets like stocks, then it would be a lot more difficult to spend the money impulsively.

As soon as you have a considerable amount in your savings account, think about where to invest your money. Ensure that you get proper guidance from your parents or a professional to avoid getting scammed. Investing your money not only prevents you from spending, but it can also increase the value of the money over time.

- **Control your big spending**

During your budgetary phase, you should have a list of all of your big spending, including rent and any other expensive things that you would need. Pay for those first to avoid needing money for them later on.

There can be many hindrances to your saving journey, depending on your previous spending habits. You have to discover these yourself and come up with suitable alternatives. It is like a vegan transitioning from meat to a non-meat diet. At first, until they fully transition, they try to find food that tastes like meat but isn't meat.

If you have to cut down on purchasing luxury items, you should. Instead of buying multiple luxury items, you could buy one after every month of consistent savings and use them at intervals.

Finally, think of managing your money as a way of taking care of yourself. Use the money you have allocated for the month wisely so you have no reason to reach into your savings. Every time you think of using your savings, remind yourself that this is for your success and personal growth. You can't cheat yourself if you want good results.

The ultimate goal is to be the best version of yourself, and financial responsibility is a must.

As we're about to discuss investing in the next chapter, ensure that you trust yourself and believe that you can do it, and you will become a more financially intelligent person.

CHAPTER 4

Introduction to Investing

A common misconception is that investing is only for adults or grownups. The truth is, there is no age too young or too old for investing. In fact, some parents invest by using the names of their kids after they are born so they can benefit from it in the future.

If you saved up to $1000 worth of money from your allowance, Christmas, and other holiday money gifts for a year, you might not know what to do with the money because your parents provide everything you need. You can keep that money until you need it, but its value will not increase over time. It will always be $1,000. However, if you invest the money into something that would bring a profit in another year, it can grow to $2,000, $3000, and even $10,000, depending on how good your investment was.

Investing is when you use your money to buy things that will bring you profit in the future. When you buy things such as paintings, Pokémon cards, or Manga collections that have an increasing value with the aim of selling them for a higher price in the future and making more money, that is an investment.

Aside from the things mentioned above, there are so many items and businesses you can invest in, especially at this young age, and we'll be discussing all of them in this chapter. The primary goal of investment is to get profit after some time, and there is no minimum or maximum amount required for an investment.

Understanding Investing and Its Basics

When you spend money on food or drinks with friends, you consume them immediately, and the money is gone too. However, with investing you spend money, but the money isn't gone. Whatever you use your money for will, in turn, make money for you in the future. With this logic, you can say, for instance, that getting a new laptop because you want to write a book is an investment.

Over time, you will write your book, and when your book gets published, you can make a lot more money from it than the cost of one laptop. In the same way, buying a camera for your YouTube channel is also an investment because if the quality of your content gets you more viewers, then that will set you on your way to monetization. Over time, the money you make will surpass the cost of the camera you bought.

Deciding to invest your money should mean that you have no immediate use for the money. Investments work better when you leave your money to build value in the long term. This means that you will get more money if you let your investment remain working for you longer. If you need the money back in six months, then you'd be better off either finding short investments or not investing the money at all.

However, with short-term investments, you will not make as much profit as with long-term ones, and you are more exposed to risks. Investing works only if you have the money to invest. Ensure that the money you want to invest is available before starting.

Don't jump into investing in everything, especially if you are not sure of your investment options. You can start by dedicating a percentage of your savings so that you still have something to fall back on in case of loss. Investing all your savings can put you at risk of losing it if your investment goes sideways.

Before investing in anything, ensure that you do proper research and ask a professional and an adult for guidance. If it is something minor, such as Pokémon cards, you may not need adult help. Buy the card that has the rarest value because it will become even rarer over time.

It may be difficult to find a business with profit potential on your own, so you can start small by investing in a place that serves people constantly. That way, you will be on the path to making daily profits based on the amount of your investment.

Making long-term investments does not mean you should forget about them. If you do, your investment may be at risk. You have to be up-to-date on things happening where your investment is. That way, you know when it is best to get your profits back. Constantly checking the value of your investment will tell you if you can add more money or reduce the money you have invested.

The Importance of Starting Early

Some companies started when you were born. At that time, buying stocks and shares in that company might have cost as little as $10. With that one purchase, fast forward to 13 years later; that $10 might be worth $1,000 or more. Now imagine if you invested more. That is basically what investing does. Your investment has the potential to bring you a lot more profits than you imagine, depending on how the market is doing.

As mentioned at the beginning of this chapter, there is no age too young to invest. Starting your investment at a young age may be what gives you financial stability in your 20s and 30s. After saving a part of your allowance or earnings, you can choose to invest some of that money. The investment can become useful to you in five years or more.

The most important reason to start investing young is that the sooner you invest, the earlier you take control of your financial future. If you invest at 13 years old, imagine how much money you will have when you are 18 and living on your own. Even without a job, you may have made enough money to get a car or afford some college expenses your parents can't pay for immediately.

Investing at a young age also shows maturity and builds good saving habits. If you can save and invest early, you'll have no problems doing it when you are older. When you start early, you learn more about investing as you go, including the best places to invest compared to the risk of investment. You will easily recover from losses and have a better understanding of investment risks.

The risk of investing is manageable when you start early because you can easily make money back if hit with a loss. You're young; time is on your side, and you have more time to recover than if you were in your 40s or 60s. If your investment yields profits over the years, you become more financially stable, and your financial responsibilities will be reduced.

When you invest at a young age, you can avoid working multiple jobs to survive when you're in your 20s because you have something to fall back on. However, if you wait until you are in your 20s to invest, the money will not yield profit overnight.

Risks and Rewards of Investing

Investing is when you put your money into different things with the hope of making more money over time. While investing can be a great way to grow your wealth, it's important to be aware of the risks and rewards involved. Let's explore the different risks and rewards of investing so you can make informed decisions about your financial future.

Potential Rewards:

- **Growth**: Investing can help you grow your wealth over time. Stocks, bonds, and real estate have historically provided higher returns than traditional savings accounts or CDs.

- **Income**: Some investments, such as dividend-paying stocks, bonds, and rental properties, can provide a steady stream of income.

- **Building Wealth**: As a teenage investor, one of your goals is to build wealth. Whether you want to save for emergencies or college, investing can give you a head start on the future you want.

- **Diversification**: Investing allows you to spread your money across different asset classes, industries, and geographic regions. This can help reduce the risk of loss and smooth out volatility.

- **Beating Inflation**: Investing can help you stay ahead of inflation, which erodes the purchasing power of your money over time.

- **Career Flexibility**: Investing can give you the flexibility and options you desire in your future career choices. When you have a solid investment portfolio, you'll feel empowered to fuel your passions and explore entrepreneurial opportunities without being fully dependent on traditional employment for support.

Potential Risks:

- **Market Volatility**: The value of investments can fluctuate widely in response to changes in economic conditions, market sentiment, and other factors.

- **Loss of Principal**: Unlike savings accounts or CDs, investments are not guaranteed to preserve your initial capital. You may experience losses, sometimes substantial, especially in the short term.

- **Lack of Diversification**: It can be risky to put all your eggs in one basket. Concentrating your investments in a single stock, sector, or asset class exposes you to greater risk if that investment performs poorly.

- **Inflation Risk**: While investing can help you beat inflation over the long term, there's always the risk that inflation could outpace your investment returns.

Investing money may be as easy as putting money into an asset, but it comes with risks. Although the profit from long-term investments is greater, there is always a risk of losing money, especially with short-term investments. So, it is always advisable to invest your money for the long term (minimum 5 years) to get better results.

So, are you still contemplating investing? I'd say you should go for it—there's a whole world of financial rewards waiting for you. The saying, "The early bird gets the worm" couldn't be more true when it comes to investing. When you start investing early, you're giving your money time to expand. It's like planting a seed and watching it grow over time.

Imagine having the freedom to pursue your passions without worrying about money. Well, investment offers that freedom. You can create a source of passive income that will support you for years to come. You'll learn valuable life skills such as planning, goal-setting, and delayed gratification. You'll be financially responsible and independent. Won't it be pretty impressive when it's specified on your resumes and applications?

By starting investment early, educating yourself, and taking a long-term approach, you set yourself up for a lifetime of financial independence. So, what are you waiting for? Get started and reap the rewards!

How to Start Investing (Stocks, Bonds, Mutual Funds, and Index Funds)

The first step is to decide where to invest your savings. Considering the risk isn't something you should rush, so take your time to weigh your options using the money you have at hand as your deciding factor.

Are you ready to dip your feet into the world of finance as a future investor? There are several long-term investment options, the most popular of which are stocks, bonds, mutual funds, and index funds.

I remember the first time I heard about investing. I was in my early teens, and the word sounded so mystical and intimidating. But trust me, it's not rocket science. This topic might get you interested in the wide world of stocks, bonds, mutual funds, or index funds, but don't worry. I've got your back. Let's break it down step by step:

Stocks

Think of stocks like owning a part of your favorite company, whether it's Netflix, Apple, Nike, or Coca-Cola. When you buy stocks, you're thinking, *I believe in this company's performance, and they will succeed, so I want to be a part of it.*

Investing in stocks can be exciting when you know your investments have the potential to earn you lots of money over time. Imagine watching your investment grow as the company thrives! It was one of the things that got me listening to the news as a teenager, and I formed a habit over time.

But there's a catch—stocks can be volatile and get a bit wild. Prices can swing up and down dramatically like a pendulum, especially in the short term. So, it's important to be prepared for some roller-coaster rides along the way.

Bonds

I want you to think of bonds as loaning money to either the government or a big corporation. In return, these organizations promise to pay you back the money you loaned, plus some extra cash (interest), at a later date.

Unlike stocks, bonds are slow and steady. You might not see

huge gains immediately, but what they offer is stability and predictability.

I call bonds the responsible, low-risk finance option in the investing world. They're perfect for those who prefer a smoother ride, even if it means sacrificing some potential excitement.

Mutual Funds

Let's assume mutual funds are like a potluck dinner where different people bring in a dish. Instead of investing your entire savings in a single stock or bond, you pool your money with those of many other investors to buy a variety of investments.

One of the best parts is that the fund manager is in charge of selecting particular stocks and bonds, so you don't have to worry about that. They ensure that everything is perfectly balanced and tasty because they are the cooks in the investment kitchen.

You may instantly diversify your investments with mutual funds, which helps to spread out the risk. So even if one investment isn't performing so well, you've got plenty of others to pick up the slack.

Index Funds

Think of index funds as an easy click or option for investing. The strategy here is that rather than trying to outperform the market by selecting particular stocks, you simply aim to mirror its performance.

Index funds follow certain market indexes, such as the S&P 500, which tracks the performance of 500 of the top corporations in the United States. They are ideal for those who prefer a hands-off approach to investing. Plus, they frequently have lower costs than actively managed funds, allowing you to keep more of your hard-earned money.

Before you dive in, it's important to understand the fundamentals. The steps to start investing are as follows:

1. Learn the basics

This is the most important step, as you need to have a solid understanding of how the stock market works before you start putting your money at risk. You can learn about stock investing by reading books and articles or watching videos. There are also plenty of online courses that can teach you the basics of stock investing.

2. Identify investments that are appropriate for teenagers

There are a few different types of investments that are good for teenagers, including stocks, mutual funds, and U.S. savings bonds. Stocks are a good option for teenagers who are willing to take on some risk in exchange for the potential of higher returns. Mutual funds are a good option for teenagers who want to invest in a diversified portfolio of stocks without having to pick individual stocks. U.S. savings bonds are a good option for teenagers who are looking for a safe place to park their money.

3. Learn what the companies do

Before you invest in a company, it's important to understand what the company does and how it makes money. You can learn about a company by checking its website and reading its annual report, which is a public document that companies are required to file with the Securities and Exchange Commission (SEC). You can also learn about a company by reading its 10-K filing, which is a more detailed version of the annual report.

4. Get and use financial data

Once you know what companies you're interested in investing in, you need to start gathering financial data about the companies. This data will help you evaluate the companies and make informed investment decisions. You can find financial data about companies on their websites, on financial websites, and in financial publications.

5. Experiment with dummy or mock portfolios

One way to get started investing is to set up a dummy or mock portfolio. This is a simulated portfolio that you can use to practice investing without risking any real money. There are a few different sites that allow you to set up dummy portfolios, such as MockPortfolios.com, MarketWatch Virtual Stock Exchange, and Wall Street Survivor.

6. Choose the right custodial brokerage account for teens

As a minor, you can't open a brokerage account on your own. You need to have a parent or guardian open a custodial brokerage account for you. A custodial brokerage account is an account that's owned by a minor, but the custodian (the parent or guardian) has control over the investments in the account.

7. Avoid investment scams

There are a lot of investment scams out there, so it's important to be careful when you're investing. If someone promises you a profit that is much higher than you can get by investing in the stock market each year, you should run away, unless you really know what you're doing or you don't mind losing your money quickly. High profit in any investment usually involves much higher risk.

Now that you know the steps, you are fully ready to start investing. The next step is the most important, and that is talking to your parents or legal guardian about your decision to start investing. This is because a minor can't have a stock brokerage account without the supervision of a legal guardian.

In an agreement with your parent or legal guardian, they would open a stock brokerage account for which they would have shared custody until you are of legal age. In the same way, if you decide to invest in bonds, you will still need your parent's guidance to work with any market dealer. This is to protect you from the risk of getting scammed.

Some people may want to take advantage of the fact that you are young, so be vigilant. After your parents register for a custodial brokerage account, they will help you work with online brokers to get you the stock you want to invest in. If there are companies you are interested in, you can tell your parents, and they will help you check the companies.

Simple Investment Strategies for Beginners

As a first-time investor, you will need some strategies that will help you get the most out of your investment. Your investment amount doesn't have to be huge, so these strategies work well with small ventures. Even if your parents are in charge of the account, it is still your investment out of your savings, so you can decide on the strategy you want to use. Your strategy shouldn't be too complex since you are just starting.

- **Invest in the things you know about**

It could be the game you play, the company that makes the toys you play with (such as Lego), or a company that makes dresses you love. Since they are in your interest, you should pay more attention to the news around them. When deciding to invest, you should also consider the company's current market value.

- **Check if the company is likely to remain popular for the next few years**

You can also try a strategy called the dollar cost strategy. This is when you invest a set amount over a period. Let's say you invest $20 consistently every month. With this strategy, you can also buy stocks at low costs and then sell them at a higher price.

A good example is that you can buy a rare Lego set for $200, even better when it comes with a rare character, and after three years, you sell it for $1,000 or more, depending on how much that set is worth. The limit to how much of your savings you should invest depends on your goals for investing. Also, there will be ups and downs, so don't take it to heart.

- **Buy and hold your stock, bonds, or funds**

This is the easiest strategy for beginners, and it may be the best for young people. This way, you don't have to check on it every single day. Buying and holding have everything to do with keying into the right investment. If you make the wrong investment, you will not get good profits, and no matter how long you wait, you might end up with a loss.

- **Invest in assets that have rising value**

For example, the value of real estate properties tends to rise over time, so that would be a good place to buy and hold. While holding, you have to have a mild knowledge of how the market works, so try to read up on whatever you can about the investments.

- **Read to understand more about investment risk**

Don't make a new decision with your investment after reading rumors online. That will bring you greater risk. Make every move carefully until you can invest very well. Weigh your options logically and seek guidance when necessary.

The Concept of Compound Interest and Its Power

We can't talk about investment and not talk about compound interest since it is a term you will hear often. So, let's discuss this concept, which is very important in the finance sector. It will be a topic of much discussion, particularly concerning investments. Rest assured, though, it's not as complicated as it seems.

What's Compound Interest?

To a teenager, I usually describe compound interest as a money magic trick, similar to a magician pulling out rabbits from a single hat. It's the interest you earn on both your original investment money and the interest that's already piled up over time.

How Does it Work?

Let's break it down with an example: Say you invest $50 and assume you're earning a 10% compound interest rate. After the first year, you'd earn $5 in interest, which is 10% of $50, bringing your total to $55. But here's where it gets even cooler—in the second year, you're not just earning interest on your original $50, you're also earning it on that extra $5 you made in the first year. Now your investment will start with a new total of $55 (your original $50 plus the $5 interest added in the first year) and will earn another $5.50 (10% of $55). So, after two years, the value of your investment has jumped from $50 to $60.50. And it will keep growing (compounding) from there.

Why Does It Matter?

Understanding how compound interest works is like having a secret code for growing your money. The more you invest and the longer you leave it untouched, the more your money can grow. All you need is time.

If you start investing early, then you can use the power of compound interest to your advantage. With each passing month or year, your investment is growing while you wait for the right time to enjoy the reward of it. Compound interest will help you build wealth from a young age. The earlier you start, the better your wealth will grow.

Now that you know about the power of compound interest, let's navigate the digital money world in the next chapter.

CHAPTER 5

Navigating the Digital Money World

Digital money is real money. It is a monetary option that isn't cash. A perfect example is the money you have in your bank account that you can transfer to another person through an app on your phone. On your phone, it is just a number, but you can send a fraction of that number to someone and pay for things without having to touch cash. As long as you don't need to use cash, then it is digital money.

Here is an analogy to help you understand digital currency. Think of the games you've played. Some of them would give you coins as rewards for finishing a task or level. Later on in the game, they would show you the things you can buy with those coins. Some of these items could be extra life points, boosters, or other helpful features for the levels ahead. These coins may only work within the game and are not able to be converted to a currency that's acceptable in the real world, but they still count as digital money. The coins are usable for any purchases made in the game, which makes them currency created for exchange in that game. There could be games, however, that do allow you to exchange their coins for your primary currency.

Exploring Digital Banking

The world of digital money was created thanks to technology. What started as paper tokens turned into cash, and from cash, we have something cooler. Before the invention of digital banking, the closest thing to it was making a wire transfer, and that was only possible if you went to the bank and let the bankers do it for you.

However, that wasn't the only requirement. You also need to send a large amount of money. It's safe to say this feature was mostly used by people with huge earnings. With the invention of the smartphone, technology rose to the point where people began creating apps that you could use on your phone to manage things.

That must have been fun and groundbreaking. For example, the only way we could write words was with a pen and paper or the word software on a computer. But after the smartphone was invented, you could take notes on your phone. Now, with the advanced features of your smartphone, you can write and edit an entire essay or research paper without needing your laptop.

It sure makes life easier and more fun, and if you forget to do your assignment while out with friends, you can start doing it on your phone instead of waiting till you get home. People didn't always have such privileges. In the same way, there was an old-fashioned way to send money without having to do a physical money transfer.

This process required you to go to your bank and ask them to send money to the person of your choice. However, compared to today's method, that process was incredibly slow. The person could wait the whole day and not get the money you sent. So, what if it was an emergency? What if your friend was stranded and urgently needed money? And imagine having to take a bus to the bank and stand in line for your turn.

As many apps were being invented, people started to wonder, *What if there was a way to send money to people at any time I wanted, without having to go to the bank?* The person who thought of the idea envisioned it to be like sending a text message. If we could send money the way we send text messages, imagine how much easier it would be to make purchases without cash.

This thought is what gave birth to online banking. Banks began to provide some of their services online for their customers. Later on, a mobile application was created to reduce website traffic when transactions were made. Now, you can download your bank app on your phone and transfer money whenever you want to. The first apps were slow, but now the transactions are so fast that after you send someone money, they can receive it in less than a minute.

Initially, this sounded like magic, but it took a lot of hard work to get here. I'm not saying digital banking is perfect.

There are many ways it can be improved. For example, transaction accuracy is much better than it used to be.

What most people don't know is that using bank cards such as debit or credit cards is a part of digital banking. Remember I said that any payment made or received without cash is a digital currency? It is digital because you don't have to hold the cash in your hand physically. As online banking became popular, more applications, such as apps that can help you save money, were invented. These apps only require you to have an account with them, and you can transfer money from your bank account into the app, to be held until a date of your choosing. We discussed this in chapter 3.

Aside from these, many other mobile payment apps have come along, including one of the most popular—Apple Pay. Using Apple Pay to pay for items counts as mobile banking because there's an app on your phone rather than cash in your hand. Apple Pay became wildly popular with the use of the iPhone, but it was mostly because of its fast and efficient payment method.

People like the idea of paying for things without typing out the account details every time they want to make a new transaction. They also like the idea of not carrying their bank cards everywhere they go. All you need to do is scan a code and swipe your phone over a machine, and you are good to go. It saves a lot of time, especially for people who are in a hurry.

While Apple Pay is very popular, it's not the only mobile baking option available. You can explore the good ones and decide which ones to go with if you don't want to use the same platform as everyone else.

Another part of online banking you should know about is the digital wallet. It works like a real wallet. Just as you have a physical wallet for storing your cash so it doesn't get lost in your bag, a digital wallet is a place where you can keep track of your digital money. Sometimes your mobile app can function as a digital wallet, but what happens when you have multiple accounts with different banks? In this case, the only platform that can help you track your funds is a digital wallet.

There are many wallet apps to choose from depending on the currency in which you want to store your money. Yes, digital wallets allow you to store money in more than one currency. This can be especially helpful if you have friends and family outside the country you want to send money to, or someone who sends money to you.

Staying Safe Online

Online safety is very important in this day and age. You have a lot more to lose if your phone ever gets hacked. In the past, you would have to worry only about embarrassing pictures getting leaked, but now you have to think about the possibility of your mobile bank app getting hacked. Scammers are very smart; they are always evolving their tricks to get you to fall into their trap. But there are ways you can protect yourself.

The following are tips on how to stay safe online:

- **Get that firewall app now**

If your parents told you using a firewall app can protect you, they were right, and you should get a good one installed. However, these scammers have tricks they can use to get past your firewall. They could send you messages or emails that are disguised as things concerning you, and as you click their link on them, you will unknowingly help create a hole in your firewall, giving them the access they need to rob you.

- **Learn how to spot scam calls and text messages**

For scam calls, someone could call you pretending to be from your bank. While your bank can call you to inform you of new changes or services, they would never ask for your bank-sensitive details over the phone or via email.

A bank will never call to ask you about things involving your card lock pin, the numbers on your card, the security code of your card, or the password to your mobile app. As soon as you get calls that do ask for any of these, hang up, screenshot the number to report them to your bank, and then block the number from calling you again. Some scammers might call, asking you to subscribe to their services while they try to find an entry into your firewall. You must not stay on that call for too long. Hang up.

As for text messages and emails, when you see something suspicious, delete them. Don't click on any links, even if they may be things you genuinely want to buy. The links may take you to the item you see, but they also have created a hole in your firewall, giving the scammer access to your phone.

- **Use very strong passwords**

Don't use your birthday, nickname, or something obvious as your password. Besides scammers, there could be someone else who could get access to your account if they know you on a personal basis, and we don't want that. Make sure that your password is something no one can guess, but at the same time, it should be something you can remember. A tip for creating passwords is to use a mix of letters, numbers, and symbols. Your password will be a lot harder to guess or break if you mix it up this way.

- **Turn your connections off until you need them**

Another very important tip for your online financial security is to keep your Wi-Fi and Bluetooth connections off. If your Bluetooth isn't connected to any service, keep it off. When you keep it on, it can allow nearby scammers to connect to your phone, conduct their business, and leave your account emptied out. Be very conscious about keeping your Wi-Fi off as well.

- **Don't just connect**

In the same way, you should be mindful of the Wi-Fi you connect to, as not every free Wi-Fi service is safe. When you visit a cafe and you want to use their Wi-Fi, you can confirm the Wi-Fi address with a waitperson. Don't make the mistake of guessing and falling into the trap of a scammer. They may not be targeting you, but what would you expect them to do if you fell into their trap on your own?

These tips may seem as if you only need to protect your phone, but remember that mobile banking doesn't work with your phone alone. If you ever have to search for your card or have lost your wallet where it is stored, call your bank and have them freeze your card until it's found. If your wallet is found by someone who won't give it back, that person can empty your bank account. This is why it is important to call the bank immediately when you notice your card is missing. You don't have to wait for the next day. For things like this, most banks have 24-hour emergency services, so give them a call to save your funds.

Back to scam emails, they could be very hard to detect, so you have to confirm every web address before clicking on it. If you are careless, you can easily become a victim.

Taking your money is not the only thing these scammers can do. Some are skilled enough to install spyware on your phone, which, without your consent, mirrors every action you take. By doing this, they would be able to guess your habits and send a stronger link that will appeal to you—clicking on it could give them a way to eventually empty your bank account.

Keep in mind that some of these scammers take precautions to avoid getting caught. It can take weeks to months to plan for a heist on your account, especially if you have a lot of money saved. You have to do your best to protect yourself all the time. The moment you notice something strange on your phone, take proactive measures.

The Rise of Cryptocurrencies

When I used games to explain the concept of digital currency, I'm sure you must have wondered why no games can transfer their coins into real money. Well, someone else did, too. As mentioned before, mobile banking isn't perfect yet. For starters, there are many restrictions involving the transfer of money, especially internationally.

This means that it may take a few seconds to send money to your friends in your classroom, but it will take forever to send money to your friends outside the country. If you're wondering why it takes so long to send money, it is because of the restrictions put in place by the government. These restrictions will stop you from sending or receiving money from certain countries. Transferring funds was getting so difficult that someone thought of a way we could do it without traditional banks.

A group of people came together and thought, *What if we didn't need the bank to send money?* Even when making a mobile transfer or paying with your card, your bank is still involved because the funds come out of your bank account. So, what if you didn't have to deal with the bank? What if there was a currency other than dollars or traditional currencies that could be accepted as money? What if you could make your own currency?

These questions eventually led to the creation of cryptocurrencies, which became a leading force in digital currencies and the digital economy as a whole. I'm sure you realize that it is not easy to create a currency that will have value to anyone other than its creator. Just as the coins in your game are only relevant from within the game, you could say the same for cryptocurrencies when they were first created.

Cryptocurrencies had no monetary value for a while, but soon a lot more people started investing in them the way they would buy bonds. Cryptocurrencies started having value in the real world, but they still needed a place to be useful without conversion. That place is called the blockchain. It is more than space, though, and it feels like a whole new digital world where anything can be real, including digital money.

Lately, the blockchain has advanced to a world of multiple possibilities. There are now hundreds of cryptocurrencies, the most popular being Bitcoin. Aside from Bitcoin, there are several cryptocurrencies you can invest in. The blockchain creates a virtual marketplace for cryptocurrencies, which allows for the rise and fall in the value of various currencies.

This opened many doors for cryptocurrencies to be a good way to save money.

Depending on the market, you could earn a lot of interest from holding cryptocurrencies. Digital currencies improved transaction accuracy and speed, and they had little to no restrictions. Several times, the banks considered banning them for this reason, but soon they became too important to ban.

Now the banks have no choice but to step up their game or get left behind. Just as you would be taking risks by investing in stocks, you could still have to take risks when investing in cryptocurrency, but it is an option to consider.

The process of cryptocurrency is easy to understand. Transactions are verified on the blockchain, making them easy to track. This way is safer because your funds won't be untraceable. The blockchain acts as a journal that records a ledger of all your trades and transactions, including all the assets you have on the blockchain.

Yes, you can invest in assets on the blockchain. Very recently, you may have heard of NFTs and how they would change the lives of arts all over the world. So many of them have lost their value now, but if there is a reevaluation of the arts, NFTs can be strong enough to hold more value later. Using cryptocurrencies, you can make investments and purchases very quickly and easily. It would be as easy as buying something in your favorite game.

If you are considering investing in cryptocurrency, the first step would be getting a digital wallet app that supports cryptocurrency. You should pick one that can show you the market value of cryptocurrencies so that you can decide which ones to invest in. Before putting your money in, do a mid-research on the currencies and possibly ask a professional for advice so you don't end up losing too much money.

There is no time limit for learning more about cryptocurrencies and the investment options they give you. They can earn you a lot of interest, but you can also lose a lot of money because the market can fluctuate. However, just as with bonds, some currencies are the equivalent of your local currency. They don't move with the market value but with the real-world market value of those currencies.

Cryptocurrencies basically remove the need for a bank as a third party when you make a transaction with someone. Now, you can send money directly without any restriction as long as your partner has the same access to cryptocurrencies. The only restrictions that exist are that some networks are slower than others, and there are still some countries that are not accepting cryptocurrencies.

This is not strange at all. After all, some apps are also restricted in some countries, and some games can't be played in other countries. For example, the most popular League of Legends can't be played in some African countries, and the UEA does not allow internet calls such as WhatsApp or FaceTime calls.

As you wrap up this journey through the digital money world, be confident in your knowledge so you can thrive in a digital economy like ours. From exploring digital banking and staying safe online to living in the world of cryptocurrencies, you are well-equipped to navigate this ever-increasing digital economy with ease and confidence!

The next chapter will be discussing money management skills every teen girl should have. Stay with me!

CHAPTER 6

Mastering Money Management Skills

When you have money, whether it's your first paycheck or your monthly allowance, how you spend it says a lot about you. If the first thought that comes to you is to spend it all on clothing, shoes, makeup, or any other trendy item you feel a compulsion to get, then you lack basic financial discipline.

A person with sound financial management makes wise decisions with their money since they are aware that it won't last forever. It's similar to making a strategy for your financial expenses and savings or to the daily to-do list you make every morning before heading out. In the same way, that list helps you keep track of all you are to do so you can commit your energy only where needed. Sound financial discipline limits your spending and helps you focus on what's really important.

Rather than blowing all you get on makeup or fashionable clothes the moment you receive it, consider your objectives. Perhaps you want to put money aside for a major purchase such as a new phone or a trip with friends. Being financially disciplined is sticking to your plan and stifling the need to make hasty purchases. It also entails budgeting, which is calculating your income and allocating it to various areas such as spending, saving, and sometimes even charitable contributions.

Being financially disciplined means you're responsible with your money. Although it may not sound very exciting, it does position you for a more secure future in which you will be free to pursue your passions. Also, it feels fantastic to reach your objectives since you've been frugal and diligent with your money!

That's not all you stand to gain when you are financially disciplined. You stand to gain many other skills, knowledge, and benefits that will be useful to you in other aspects of your life. It is even believed that financial discipline improves your mental and physical health. That sounds absurd, but it's totally true. Let's find out the importance of financial discipline.

The Importance of Financial Discipline

Taking the pains to become a financially disciplined girlie sets you up for a smarter future because you undergo mental shifts that are crucial for survival and thriving in the not-so-distant future. You acquire skills and mental shifts that boost your debut in the labor market and, finally, you may be placed in positions not common to your age bracket.

Financial discipline makes you a goal-oriented person. You're not one to roam around aimlessly. You always have your eyes on new milestones, new saving goals, and new high-priority purchases. It creates a mental fix in you that sets appropriate priorities. You're not one to be swayed by the tide. You stand on business for as long as you have to. This is arguably one of the topmost-rated skills for boss-girl leaders. If you start practicing it now, you'll be a leader among your peers.

Along with this head start toward leadership roles, financial discipline also takes away headaches such as debts. A financially disciplined girl knows better than to get into financial commitments that are unnecessary and beyond the coverage of her present paycheck. She wouldn't encounter debts because she only spends within her means, not outside of them. This builds accountability and reliability; these are also top-rated skills for leaders all over the world.

Furthermore, financial discipline kickstarts a chain reaction of other disciplined mindsets and soft skills that solidify the concrete journey to wealth. You can be sure you're on your way to being a wealthy girl when you adopt good skills such as financial discipline. Borrowing this analogy from the Bible, *if you do well with little, you'll do well with many*. It's not rocket science. Skills such as financial discipline are magnets that attract all their benefits in due time.

They say a great leader stays calm in the midst of chaos. It may sound far-fetched, but financial self-control over time molds your brain and entire reasoning to an extent that emergencies don't unnerve you anymore. This quality is a result of learning to turn a deaf ear to all the external and internal compelling forces that push you to spend impulsively. This discipline builds the ability to ignore frenzied trending items and save instead.

Finally, what we can't control gives us a lot of headaches indeed. However, when you're in charge of your finances, that worry is automatically deflated. Financial discipline puts you in charge of your money so that you know what to do and don't have to stress about all the noise going on around you. This is how financial discipline impacts your health. It's safe to say that one needs financial discipline for a stronger and stress-free mindset.

Overall, financial discipline sets you up for success in life by helping you make smart decisions with your money, both now and for the future. It's a skill that pays off big time! However, it's one thing to be financially disciplined, and it's another thing to do it right. You could be planning properly but planning with the wrong goals in mind. Getting in charge of your finances typically makes you filter your pressing needs from your raging wants. So, how do you tell which is a need and which is a want?

Understanding Needs Vs. Wants

Understanding the difference between needs and wants is a fundamental part of financial discipline. It makes the whole process rewarding and fulfilling. Just as a car needs fuel and oil to function properly, you need to understand the difference between wants and needs to make the most rewarding use of financial discipline. The thin line between needs and wants is often hard to see, but there's a trick to better understanding the two.

The trick is to ask yourself one simple question: *Do I need this thing to survive?* If the answer is "yes," then it's a need. If the answer swings between "maybe" and "not now," then it is a want. If the answer is a firm "no," trash the thought immediately. It is an unnecessary want.

There are other tricks for figuring out needs and wants. Needs can be grouped under the umbrella of things that are needed to continue and survive in the course of life, while wants can be grouped under attachments.

Needs such as food, health care, education, and transportation can't be negotiated, so they must get a fair allocation of the money you've got in hand. They are like the necessary bolts and nuts—the ball joints that need to be tightened firmly for the smooth running of the car. If they're lacking in any way, without proper oiling for instance, they could cause friction. That friction would, in turn, cause avoidable wear and tear that would eventually make driving the car unsafe.

Ignoring your needs can directly impair your health. When you think of something you have to spend your money on, think of the long-term effects if you neglect it. If the effects could stunt your physical or psychological growth, then it is a need, and you shouldn't ignore it. These would be things such as a soft-skill improvement course, a pair of prescription glasses, and a new laptop—things that are either a replacement for faulty old ones or first installments because a lack has been identified.

Your wants, on the other hand, are simple desires and

wishes. These are things that you'd like to have but aren't essential for survival. They include entertainment, hobbies, trendy items, and luxuries. Most times, we start yearning for these things because they're popular among our friends. The easiest way to identify a want is to ask yourself the first question I asked earlier. *If I don't get this thing you desire, would it hurt me in any way?*

The amazing thing about wants is that they may appear cheaper than our needs, so we indulge them a little too much and then realize, when it's a little too late, that we've spent so much on unnecessary things. Wants can have a compelling urge in our minds, but if you take the pains to ignore them, you'll reap the fruits soon enough. The money saved from ignoring our wants can be invested into more rewarding needs.

Needs are like an investment that yields results sooner or later. Good health keeps your body strong so you can achieve more. Sound education yields a proper career takeoff. A good haircut boosts the confidence necessary for social skills. Wants, on the other hand, have a very temporary value-return. A Versace watch gets you high with pride and the feeling of belonging among wealthy friends this minute, and the next minute, you're by yourself—broke and upset that you spent so much for the watch.

This is not to say that entertainment such as social gatherings with friends should be ignored. You do need social skills to make progress in your career and as a person. However, it shouldn't be a regular thing. Also, you don't need to be in on every social gathering. And not all social gatherings are beneficial to your overall growth. You're hurting your future if you're hitting the club on back to back nights at such a tender age as this. As early as now, filtering your social gatherings is very important.

Ultimately, it's important to have a long and serious conversation with yourself. Filtering your needs from your wants, allocating adequate funding to your needs, and setting your wants aside will make financial discipline worthwhile. You start to prioritize your spending.

Financial discipline involves meeting your needs first before indulging in wants. It's about ensuring that you're allocating your resources (money, time, and energy) in a way that aligns with your values and long-term goals. By distinguishing between needs and wants, you can make informed decisions that lead to greater financial stability and satisfaction.

Tips for Spending Wisely and Avoiding Impulse Buys

Now that you've had that important conversation with yourself, you can separate your wants from your needs. The next step is taking charge of the urge to get unnecessary things. Though the human mind works wonderfully, your will isn't enough to become totally disciplined financially. You still need an action plan; without the action plan, you fall back to square one. The human mind is programmed in such a way that often you do the exact opposite of what you should do. That's why banking on will alone won't get you far. With an action plan, your will gets fortified and finally becomes a reality.

Here are tips to help you spend wisely and avoid impulse buying:

- **Develop an action plan**

What kind of action plans would you need to actualize financial discipline? What kind of action plan puts the leash on impulse buys? The general answer is to set boundaries. There are different kinds and stages of boundaries you can set to reduce and totally take charge of impulse buys. The first step is to identify the problem. Identify those items you always buy on impulse before you head to the drawing board. Once you've identified the item, the next step is to select the kind of boundary you'll need to curtail impulsive buys.

- **Set boundaries now**

The different kinds of boundaries include budgeting, setting priorities, hold-to-think-it-over, avoidance, setting spending limits, opting for debit cards, stretching, and deep-searching. These limits can be practiced in different ways, and the sweetest part is that they're really easy to adopt.

Avoidance alone won't stop you from throwing your budget to the wind, so you'd need to take it a step further by opting for debit cards. It's easy to overshoot budgets with credit cards, but debit cards automatically limit spending ability. You could also opt for cash. This limits the money at hand, which could limit your ability to get items on impulse.

- **List your priorities**

Start by setting your priorities. This is done by separating needs from wants. Then, it is modified by setting pressing needs first before other needs. Next, you fix a budget. Allocate funds to your top priorities and move on to the next step. After fixing a certain amount of money for top needs, the next step is to place extra barriers that would stop you from throwing your budget to the wind. Identify places or things that fuel impulse buys. It could be a supermarket or an online store; just do your best to avoid them.

- **Spending limits work**

This doesn't mean you have to deprive yourself totally. You deserve to be happy, too, but spending recklessly on things that bring temporary happiness has more depressing consequences. What you can do is to set spending limits for miscellaneous items or activities. You could also practice delayed gratification; hold for a long time the urge to spend, with a promise to give in later after some amount of work or reaching a saving goal. Most times, the urge dissipates before you reach your set goal, so you get to save more.

- **Sleep on it**

Finally, if the urge is really stubborn, sleep on it. Hold the urge for at least 24 hours and think about it. Ask yourself the consequences of not getting the item and the long-term benefits of buying it. If you come up with no tangible reason, the urge will deplete after several hours. If you can't see a clear picture, that could mean this is a want that isn't worth your time and money.

How to Avoid Common Financial Pitfalls

Common financial pitfalls such as zero budgeting, credit card misuse, lack of saving, and impulse spending can be avoided if you apply some simple tricks highlighted here.

- **Start with making a budget**

Make a budget for everything, even your transportation. Save up for emergencies. When you have extra money left after a budget, don't spend it all at once. Throw it into your savings, and it will come in handy later.

- **If you can't afford it, avoid it**

If something comes up out of the blue, and you need to get it, dip your hands into your savings if you have to. However, if all your savings end up falling short of the amount of money you need, don't go on ahead to get it on credit. Don't get into debt this early. The better thing to do is negotiate installment payments.

- **Set daily spending limits**

For each day, before you step out of your home, plan ahead and set a daily spending limit. You can choose to take that set amount out in cash and keep your credit or debit cards back at home. Then, allocate some amount to at least three goals for the day. They could be transportation, lunch, and an assignment project. Carry along some loose change for emergency supplies; when those don't occur, bring it back and save it up.

- **Plan your meals**

You can plan your meals before you leave the house. Limiting the amount of time you eat out can help save you from overspending on food. If you're opting for cash, it's advisable to use your bank's atm to avoid additional charges.

- **Stay accountable**

Once you're back home, take some time out to track your expenses for the day. You could list them in a notebook and compare how you spent money with the original plan you had for the day. Whatever the results are, plan to do better the next day. Financial discipline doesn't happen overnight. It is a gradual process you grow into.

- **Check for discount offers before making a purchase**

Thankfully, we live in a digital era, so your options for discount offers aren't limited to newspapers and fine print alone. It's not that those don't work anymore—they still do, so check them out as often as you can for amazing discount deals. If you've got a smartphone, follow your favorite retailers on social media and look out for when they post discount options. If you're not into social media, or you plan to avoid it to limit impulse spending, you can sign up for newsletters that feature good deals. When you get these offers, compare them, and settle for the best ones.

- **Negotiate**

You mustn't always buy things at their asking price. There's nothing shameful about negotiating the price of any item you're interested in. If you end up getting it for some cents less, it's a good save. Discounts and negotiations help you stick to a budget and even save extra money.

Whether you're saving for something big or investing for financial freedom, the skills you've learned in this chapter will serve you. Now, go out there and embrace the power of financial literacy! Next, it's wising up on personal finance!

CHAPTER 7

Wise Up on Personal Finance

In today's fast-paced world, understanding how to manage your money effectively is crucial for achieving financial freedom and security. It seems that every other day, inflation is on the rise. Therefore, financial knowledge and skills are important for teenagers, especially girls, so you can have a better understanding of money and make it work for you. When you learn the necessary financial skills, you are better equipped and ready to stay afloat, winning even during inflation. .

Personal finance refers to the management of a person or a home's financial resources and decisions. It encompasses all the various skills highlighted in the previous chapter for financial independence. Personal finance is financial planning that includes budgeting, saving, investing, borrowing, and managing debt.

While a business is concerned with sales, an individual is concerned with optimizing financial well-being with specific goals set in mind. Personal finance is aimed toward goals like a new car, buying a home, or funding an education. It also involves careful decision-making on subjects such as income, expenses, assets, liabilities, and financial goals based on personal circumstances and priorities.

However, it doesn't stop at numbers and spreadsheets; it's about developing healthy financial habits and attitudes that support your long-term financial goals. Whether you're aiming to build wealth, achieve financial independence, or be a girl who can control her finances, this chapter will show you that something more than knowledge is needed; the practicality of the resources will provide you with the knowledge and tools needed to succeed.

We've taken several of the first steps needed to improve personal finance. With the jumpstart knowledge of budgeting, investing, and other financial schemes, you're well-prepared and on your way to learning about new aspects and components of financial literacy.

Credit Scores and Credit Cards

First, what is a credit score?

Credit scores are like report cards that show if a person is worthy of advance loans and other financial opportunities. A credit score is calculated based on your financial behavior and credit history. Lenders or banks use these scores before making a loan or giving credit to determine how much risk a borrower comes with. Higher scores typically mean better creditworthiness, and they range from 300 to 850.

Factors such as payment history, credit utilization, length of credit history, credit categories, and newly opened credit accounts are some of the factors that determine your credit score. Credit-monitoring institutions such as Equifax, Experian, and TransUnion construct that report card.

A good credit score indicates proper financial management, and it raises the possibility of receiving positive loan conditions and cheaper interest rates. On the other hand, a bad credit score is caused by late payments and high debts.

What about credit cards?

With the use of credit cards, consumers can borrow money from credit card issuers up to a predefined limit to make purchases. Users are allowed to spend up to this amount and must refund the borrowed amount by the due date. The refund usually happens monthly, and it comes with interest if it's not fully paid.

Credit cards ensure convenience and a sense of financial security. Users can make a variety of payments with them, especially daily transactions. When used properly, a credit card user gets rewards for timely payments and less debt. However, the amount of credit open to users varies. The limit is usually determined by income and credit history.

Users can only use the limited amount their history or income level allows them to borrow from. They typically refund the borrowed money at the end of a month.

Cardholders get a statement at the end of each cycle that lists all of their purchases, the total amount outstanding, and the minimum payment required.

Credit cards indeed give some financial security, but there's still that deadline for payment hovering around your head all month. By the deadline shown on the statement, cardholders must make at least the minimum payment. Interest is charged on the outstanding balance if the entire amount is not paid, resulting in further expenses.

Planning for the Future

The entire essence of this book is to help you plan better for the future. You've still got a long road ahead of you, and driving on without a plan, especially in a digital age such as this one, is risky. So you need to prearrange for college, retirement, and long-term goals. When it comes to going to college, saving for the future, and tackling long-term goals, think of it as creating a super cool game plan for your money journey!

Start by laying out your money map; figure out how much you've got coming in, where it's going, and what's left for saving. The first thing to do is create an emergency fund. Think of this as a video game. You know those coins you always have stashed away that come in handy when you're faced with a difficult situation? That's what your emergency fund serves as.

This isn't what you're used to hearing, but it makes total sense to start saving up for college now. College tuition fees can be frighteningly unreasonable, so it's wise to start saving up now, especially if you have a steady inflow of allowances or income from a side job. Even if you're unsure about going to college, saving up now will save you a lot of headaches when you change your mind in the future.

Also, there's retirement to consider. I know it sounds hasty, but it makes total sense to start thinking of retirement now. This indicates that you need a reliable financial game plan. That plan will cover your spending habits, your top priorities for the years to come, and your saving plan.

Even if you're considering starting a business after college, you need to start planning now. That plan also includes a list of skills you may want to invest in that will be necessary for your future career path. It's never too early, and it's better now when you're less burdened with college tuition and have zero debts.

In fact, this plan is necessary if you don't want to go into debt. It mustn't be a really long plan that spans years. It could be something that you try for a few months, and if it works well, you can repeat it for more months and even years. The primary goal is to highlight your long-term and short-term goals and plan around them. That would involve a lot of soul-searching.

Loans, Debts, and Financial Risks

Loans

Loans are like a financial boost that you can get from a bank or other lending institution when you need extra money for something important such as getting an education, launching a business, or buying a car. Think of it as borrowing some cash, and then you agree to pay it back later at an agreed time. It's like having a temporary allowance from a grown-up source but with a plan to return it with a bit extra, known as interest.

Interest is the cost of using someone else's money. Just as when your friend lends you their game, you've got to give it back and maybe share some extra snacks as a thank-you. Usually, you have to return the game at a specific time. When you fail to return the game or money at the agreed time, you've run into debt. That overdue payment is what is called debt.

Debts

Having debts isn't always a bad thing. There are good debts and bad debts. A good debt usually stands as an ally. It is money borrowed for a good cause, especially one that would yield good interest. These are usually debts incurred from investing in education, home mortgages, and business. Homes and buildings appreciate over time, so it is a great investment. Businesses will yield interest, too, so they are a great investment.

Bad debts refer to overdue payments for purchases with depreciating value or zero interest. This can be incurred from taking out personal loans for things such as cars and miscellaneous expenditures. Another bad debt is accumulated interest from overdue payments on credit cards. It's better not to get into debt, but if you must, it should be the kind that helps you grow, not pulls you back.

Financial Risks

Financial risk is the potential of losing the money invested in a business or decision. This is the danger of capital or money loss. After taking out loans for a business and running into good debt, there's still the danger of losing that loan.

Financial risks are somewhat inevitable and are always at the back of every businessperson's mind. It usually occurs when the money borrowed proves insufficient to meet all its obligations. There are different types of financial risks, including credit, operational, foreign investment, legal, equity, and liquidity risks.

These risks are almost inevitable. They can be managed if there's an emergency fund stashed away somewhere. Remember what I said about emergency funds earlier? They help out in situations like this. Before embarking on a business idea, ensure that you're an efficient saver with an emergency fund stashed away somewhere.

Emergency Fund

Having an emergency fund is super important in any financial plan. It's like a safety net for unexpected expenses or money problems. The main goal is to gain stability and security for when you really need it to cover things such as medical stuff, sudden repairs, or risky business situations.

The size of your emergency fund depends on your situation—how much you make, spend, and owe. Most money pros say you should save up to three to six months' worth of living costs in your emergency fund. But some say you should save even more, especially if your income is up and down or you have big financial responsibilities.

Your emergency fund needs to be easy to get to when you need it. So, it's best to keep it in accounts that you can access quickly and without extra fees—usually savings accounts or money market accounts. That way, you have easy access to your funds during an emergency.

Creating an emergency fund involves putting money aside regularly. This means saving a portion of each paycheck until you reach your savings goal. Budgeting can help you figure out where you can cut back on spending so you can save more.

Having an emergency fund is important, but having the right insurance is also crucial. Health insurance covers medical emergencies, auto insurance covers accidents, and homeowners' or renters' insurance covers property damage.

If you dip into your emergency fund for an unexpected expense, make sure to replenish it as soon as you can. This will help keep your fund strong and ready for future emergencies.

An emergency fund gives you peace of mind and stability when times get tough. By building and maintaining your emergency fund, you'll be better prepared to handle any financial challenges that come your way.

Gaining Financial Independence

Financial independence is a big deal when it comes to personal finance. It means you can afford to live the lifestyle you want without having to rely on a job or outside help. You've got enough money saved up and invested to cover your living expenses, flexible spending, and financial goals. Basically, you're free to do whatever you want with your life because you don't have to worry about money.

There are a few things you need to do to achieve financial independence. First, you need to save and invest a portion of your income over time. This will help you build a nest egg that you can use to support yourself in retirement or when you decide to leave your job. You also need to manage your debt wisely. This means paying off high-interest debt as quickly as possible so that you can free up more money to save and invest.

Another important part of achieving financial independence is spending mindfully. You need to make sure that you're not spending more than you earn. This means living below your means and cutting back on unnecessary expenses. By doing this, you can free up more money to save and invest.

Financial independence gives you the freedom to make choices based on what you want to do with your life, not what you have to do to make money. You can retire early, start your own business, travel the world, or relax and enjoy your life. However, it's important to remember that maintaining financial independence requires some risk management. You need to make sure that you're diversified enough to protect your wealth and that you have enough insurance to cover unexpected expenses.

Financial independence is a journey that takes time, discipline, and smart financial decisions. But it's a journey that's worth it. When you achieve financial independence, you'll have the freedom to live your life on your own terms and enjoy greater peace of mind.

How to Gain Financial Independence

Achieving financial independence means having enough money to live comfortably without having to work. It's a goal that many people strive for, but it isn't easy to reach. There are a few key things you can do to increase your chances of achieving financial independence.

- **Save and invest regularly**

  This is the most important thing you can do to build wealth over time. Start by setting aside a percentage of your income each month and investing it in stocks, bonds, or other assets. Over time, your investments will grow in value, and you'll be able to use them to support yourself later or pursue other financial goals.

- **Minimize debt**

  High-interest debt can eat away your savings and make it difficult to reach your financial goals. If you have debt, focus on paying it off as quickly as possible. This will free up more money for saving and investing.

- **Live within your means**

  This means tracking your expenses and making sure that you're not spending more than you earn. It also means creating a budget and sticking to it. By living within your means, you can free up more money to save and invest.

- **Generate passive income**

  Passive income streams can help you supplement your income and reach financial independence more quickly. Passive income can come from things like rental properties, dividend-paying stocks, or affiliate marketing.

- **Plan for the unexpected**

  Unexpected expenses can happen to anyone, so it's important to have an emergency fund in place. This fund should be enough to cover three to six months of living expenses.

- **Continuously educate yourself**

  The financial world is constantly changing, so it's important to stay informed about the latest trends. Read books, take online courses, and listen to podcasts to learn more about personal finance.

- **Set financial goals**

  Having clear financial goals will help you stay motivated and focused on your journey to financial independence. Whether you want to retire early, travel the world, or have more financial freedom, establishing clear goals will help you get there.

Remember that achieving financial independence takes time and effort, but it's definitely possible. Now that you have the skills that can help increase your chances of reaching your financial goals and enjoying a more financially secure future, it's time to explore entrepreneurship in the next chapter.

Profitable Business Ideas

CHAPTER 8

Exploring Entrepreneurship to Strengthen Your Financial Future

Entrepreneurship is basically all about spotting cool opportunities to start something new or shake things up in existing businesses. Entrepreneurs are the ones who are bold enough to take on the adventure of launching and running businesses, all in the hopes of making some cash and adding value.

Entrepreneurs are pretty unique folks; they've got this mix of big ideas, passion, bounce-back ability, and the capability to make things happen. They're great at spotting market gaps or problems and coming up with clever ways to fix them. Sometimes this means launching a new product, service, or business model; sometimes it's about just making existing ones better.

This chapter will teach you all about putting your ideas into action. This involves being okay with taking risks and having the vision to see possibilities where others might see roadblocks.

Benefits of Entrepreneurship for Teen Girls

Starting a business can be a game-changer for you. It's not just about making money—it's about discovering what you're capable of, following your passions, and leaving a mark on the world. By diving into entrepreneurship, you pick up crucial skills, build up resilience, and take control of your life. It sets you up for success in whatever you choose to do.

Entrepreneurship is all about empowering yourself. For teenage girls, launching a business is a chance to stand on their two feet, challenge stereotypes, and carve out their own path. By taking charge of your dreams and going all-in on what you love, you boost your confidence to tackle challenges head-on, smash through barriers, and reach your goals. This inner strength doesn't help just in business—it pushes you to speak up for yourself, chase your aspirations, and stick to it when things get tough.

Another cool thing about being an entrepreneur is the

chance to learn new stuff. Running a business means picking up a whole range of skills such as like communication, leadership, and budgeting. Teenage girls get to sharpen these skills for real, gaining hands-on experiences that'll help them crush it in any gig they choose. From pitching ideas to leading a team or managing money, they build up the practical smarts and know-how to rock in a fast-changing world.

Entrepreneurship is a hub for fresh ideas and creativity. Teenage girls bring their unique spin to the table, drawing on their experiences and insights to come up with smart solutions to big problems. By unleashing their creativity as a driving force for good, they become leaders of change, pushing society forward in smart and meaningful ways. They also learn to see failure as a natural part of the creative process, taking on challenges with power, drive, and flexibility.

Being savvy with finances is key in entrepreneurship. Building and running a business requires a good grip on money skills such as budgeting, managing cash flow, and smart investing. By getting hands-on experience in financial planning and management, these girls gain the skills to make smart choices about money, risks, and growing a business. Entrepreneurship also opens doors for them to explore funding options, giving them the tools to turn their visions into reality.

Failures are just part of the game in entrepreneurship. They're hard to dodge, but they're also golden chances for teenage girls to grow their toughness, grit, and never-give-up spirit. By seeing failure as a normal step in the game, these girls turn setbacks into lessons and fuel for the road ahead. Through trial and error, they tweak their plans, boost their processes, and up their odds of success down the line.

At the end of the day, entrepreneurship hands a heap of perks to teenage girls. It's about exploring their strengths, picking up new skills, and leaving a positive mark on the world.

10 Business Ideas for Teen Girls

1. Handmade Crafts and Artwork

If you're a teen girl with a knack for creativity and craftsmanship, you might want to check out the world of handmade crafts and artwork. There's a wide range of mediums to experiment with, from jewelry-making to painting, pottery, and more. You can create unique, one-of-a-kind pieces and sell them through various channels.

Online platforms like Etsy provide a global marketplace

where you can showcase your creations to a wide audience. Additionally, local craft fairs, markets, and pop-up events offer opportunities to connect with customers in your community.

To succeed in the handmade crafts and artwork niche, you'll need to focus on developing your skills and refining your unique style. Draw inspiration from your interests, hobbies, and personal experiences to create pieces that resonate with your target audience.

Building a strong brand identity and storytelling around your creations can help differentiate your products in a crowded market. Moreover, investing in high-quality materials and craftsmanship can enhance the perceived value of your offerings and attract discerning customers willing to pay premium prices.

2. YouTube Channel

Do you have a passion for connecting with people and creating online content? If yes, you're in luck. Recent research shows that many young girls earn impressive amounts of money from creating content for YouTube. So what are you waiting for?

Identify your niche, start engaging with your target audience, collaborate with other YouTubers, and optimize your channel for growth. Great niches to explore include food vlogging, travel, written content, DIY sustainable fashion, and life hacks. Create unique content, be dedicated and consistent, and portray a captivating personality; in no time you'll build a loyal following that generates income through views. You can monetize your channel through sponsorships, ads, and merchandise.

3. Fashion Design

If you're passionate about fashion and clothing, there are a ton of opportunities for you to explore. You can experiment with designing and creating your clothing line, incorporating your unique sense of style and creativity into your designs. You can also offer clothing alteration services, helping customers customize and personalize their existing wardrobe pieces to fit their preferences and body shapes.

Building a successful fashion business needs a mix of creativity, technical skills, and business know-how. You should invest time in learning about garment construction, fabric selection, and sewing techniques to produce high-quality garments that meet customer expectations. You can also leverage digital tools and software to create digital prototypes and visualizations of their designs, streamlining the design process and enhancing communication with clients.

In addition to creating original designs, you can explore sustainable and ethical fashion practices, such as using eco-friendly materials, upcycling thrift clothing, or implementing zero-waste production techniques. By aligning your business with values of sustainability and social responsibility, you attract environmentally conscious customers and stand out in the market.

4. Blogging

This is a great small business idea for girls who want to be their own boss. Blogging is a great way to build a professional reputation, connect with others, and establish yourself as an expert. It also allows you to work from home and avoid the daily grind of commuting, dressing up, and dealing with office politics.

If you're a good writer or even a decent videographer, you can start your blog. Blogging on social media is becoming increasingly popular. If you're interested in food or travel blogging, you can start your blog and start monetizing it once it gets some traction.

You can display ads or partner with brands to promote their products. There are plenty of platforms out there that make it easy to learn how to blog, such as WordPress.com.

5. Baking and Catering

You can offer baking and catering services for special occasions such as birthdays, weddings, and parties. Think homemade cakes, cookies, cupcakes, and all those yummy goodies that people can't resist.

To nail it in the baking and catering world, focus on honing your culinary skills. Experiment with different recipes, draw inspiration from your family's secret recipes or your favorite flavors and add your personal touch to create mouthwatering treats. Don't forget about presentation and packaging, as they play a huge role in making your food stand out. Investing in quality ingredients and stylish packaging can make your goodies even more appealing.

Also, building a strong brand is key. Use social media platforms such as Instagram and Facebook to show off your creations, connect with potential clients, and get your name out there. Consider collaborating with event planners and local businesses to expand your network and reach more customers. With a little creativity and marketing savvy, you can turn your baking hobby into a thriving business.

6. Social Media Management

If you're a tech-savvy teen and love using social media, you could offer social media management services to businesses and individuals who want to improve their online presence. You could help them create content, manage their accounts, and engage with their audience to build brand awareness, drive traffic, and generate leads.

To be successful as a social media manager, you need to stay up-to-date on the latest trends and best practices in social media marketing. You should understand the algorithms, analytics, and strategies that drive engagement and conversion. You can use your creativity and storytelling skills to develop compelling content that resonates with your client's target audience and communicates their brand message effectively.

Building a strong personal brand is essential for attracting clients and establishing credibility as a social media manager. You can showcase your expertise and portfolio through your social media channels—sharing tips, tutorials, and case studies that demonstrate your capabilities and track record of success. You can also participate in online communities, forums and networking events to connect with potential clients and collaborators.

Offering social media management services requires strong communication, organization, and time management skills. You need to be able to effectively communicate with clients, understand their goals and objectives, and translate them into actionable strategies and campaigns that deliver results. You should also be able to juggle multiple clients and projects simultaneously—prioritizing tasks and deadlines to ensure timely delivery and client satisfaction.

7. Event Planning

If you have a knack for organization and a flair for creativity, you might want to consider a career in event planning. Event planners help clients plan and coordinate all sorts of events, from weddings to parties to corporate events. They work with clients to choose a venue, develop a theme, decorate the space, arrange catering, and book entertainment. They also manage the logistics of the event, making sure everything runs smoothly from start to finish.

To be a successful event planner, you need to be able to identify your niche and target market. You need to understand the specific needs and preferences of your clients and tailor your services accordingly. You can specialize in certain types of events such as weddings or children's parties, or you could focus on serving specific demographics such as corporate clients or nonprofit organizations.

It's also important to build a strong network of vendors and suppliers. You need to be able to work with florists, caterers, photographers, entertainers, and other event professionals to create an amazing experience for your clients. You can find vendors through online directories and word-of-mouth or by attending industry events.

Finally, effective communication and collaboration are essential skills for event planners. To bring your ideas to life, you need to be able to listen to your client's needs, communicate your vision clearly, and coordinate with multiple stakeholders. You also need to be adaptable and resourceful, able to troubleshoot problems and handle unexpected challenges with grace and professionalism.

8. Photography

If you've got a thing for taking shots of people and places, you should consider going into photography. Turn your hobby into a profitable business by offering photography services to clients in your community. You can specialize in various niches, such as portrait photography, event photography, pet photography, or product photography.

To succeed as a photographer, you'll need to invest in high-quality equipment and software. You can also take courses or workshops to improve your technical skills and learn about different photography techniques.

Building a strong portfolio is essential for attracting clients. Collaborate with friends, family, or local models to create photo shoots that showcase your versatility and creativity. You can also offer discounted or pro bono sessions to build your portfolio and gain experience.

Two essential components of creating a profitable photography business are marketing and promotion. Leverage social media platforms to showcase your work, engage with followers, and attract potential clients. You can also participate in local events, contests, or exhibitions to network with other photographers and industry professionals.

9. Fitness Training

If you're passionate about fitness and wellness, you could become a certified fitness trainer or yoga instructor and offer classes or personal training sessions to clients in your community. You could specialize in various disciplines such as strength training, cardio, yoga, Pilates, or dance, depending on your interests and expertise.

To succeed in this field, you'll need to get the proper certifications and qualifications from accredited organizations. This may require completing training programs, passing exams, and getting CPR and first aid certifications. You'll also need to market yourself effectively to build a strong client base. Social media platforms such as Instagram, TikTok, and YouTube can be great ways to share workout routines, fitness tips, and motivational content with your target audience. You can also offer free or discounted trial sessions to attract new clients and get word-of-mouth referrals from satisfied customers.

Once you've established a client base, it's important to create a positive and supportive environment in which clients feel comfortable and encouraged. Focus on building relationships with your clients, understanding their goals and preferences, and providing personalized guidance and encouragement. You can also offer a variety of classes and services, flexible scheduling options, and incentives such as rewards programs or challenges to keep your clients coming back for more.

10. Environmental Services

If you're passionate about environmental conservation and sustainability, you could start a business that offers eco-friendly products or services that promote environmental awareness and management in your community. You could focus on areas like waste reduction, energy efficiency, water conservation, or sustainable living practices like composting.

To get started, you'll need to identify a specific problem or opportunity related to environmental sustainability in your community. Once you've identified a problem, you can develop a unique solution or offer to address it. This might involve conducting research, analyzing market trends, and consulting with experts or stakeholders.

Once you have a solution or offering in mind, you'll need to build partnerships and collaborations to maximize the impact and reach of your environmental initiatives. You can collaborate with local businesses, nonprofits, government agencies, and community organizations to co-create solutions, leverage resources, and mobilize collective action around shared environmental goals and objectives.

You can also engage with schools, universities, and youth organizations to raise awareness and inspire the next generation of environmental leaders and changemakers.

Marketing and promotion are essential for raising awareness of your environmental services and attracting customers. You can leverage social media platforms, community events, workshops, and educational campaigns to showcase your offerings, share success stories, and engage with potential clients and supporters. You can also participate in environmental events, fairs, or conferences to network with industry professionals, showcase your solutions, and build credibility in the field.

Overall, there is a wide range of business ideas to explore, from creative endeavors such as handmade crafts and artwork to service-based ventures such as fitness training. By leveraging interests, skills, and passions, you can turn dreams into reality and make a positive impact in your communities and beyond.

Tips for Starting a Small Business

Starting a small business can be a great way to pursue your passion, make money, and be your own boss. But it's also a lot of work. To increase your chances of success, here are some tips:

- **Get clarity**

Ask yourself these questions to get clarity. *What do I want my business to be? What problem am I solving for my customers? How am I different from my competitors?* Having a clear vision will help you stay focused and make decisions that are aligned with your goals.

- **Do your market research**

Before you start spending money or making any big decisions, take the time to research your target market, your competitors, and the industry as a whole. This will help you understand the landscape you're entering and make informed decisions about your business model.

- **Create a business plan**

A business plan is a roadmap for your business. It outlines your goals, strategies, and financial projections. It's an essential tool for any entrepreneur, as it will help you stay on track and make informed decisions about your business.

- **Secure funding**

Unless you're lucky enough to have the personal savings to fund your business, you'll need to find a way to get financing. There are a number of different options available, including loans, grants, and crowdfunding.

- **Choose the right business structure**

There are a number of different legal structures available to small businesses, each with its advantages and disadvantages. You'll need to choose the one that's right for you based on factors such as your personal liability, tax implications, and future growth plans.

- **Register your business**

Once you've chosen a business structure, you'll need to register your business with the appropriate government agencies. This will vary depending on your location, but it's an important step to ensure that your business is legal and compliant.

- **Build your brand**

Your brand is what sets you apart from your competitors. It's the sum of all the things that make your business unique, from your logo and colors to your marketing materials and customer service. Take the time to develop a strong brand identity that will resonate with your target customers.

- **Develop a marketing strategy**

Once you've built your brand, you need to develop a marketing strategy to reach your target customers and promote your products or services. There are a number of different marketing channels available, so you'll need to choose the ones that are most effective for your business.

- **Build your online presence**

In today's digital age, businesses need to have a strong online presence. This means building a professional website, being active on social media, and optimizing your website for search engines.

- **Focus on customer experience**

The best way to build a successful business is to focus on customer experience. This means delivering exceptional products and services, providing excellent customer support, and going above and beyond to meet your customers' needs.

Starting a small business is a lot of work, but it's also incredibly rewarding. By following the ideas and tips shared in this final chapter, you can increase your chances of success and build a business that you're proud of.

Conclusion

So far, you've received a load of valuable information. This isn't the time to set the book aside; it's the time to implement all you've learned. You don't need to feel overwhelmed and wonder where to start. All you have to do is write down all you've learned, set new objectives, and draw up a plan.

Draw up a budget and savings plan and follow it until you become quite used to it, and then you can plan to invest. It'll take some time to figure out your unnecessary burdens, but it's doable. Keep trying and bouncing back every time. It's never easy but very rewarding, as I've explained. Take your time to plan and talk to reliable adults around you about your plans. Talk to them about your fears and ideas.

Most importantly, practicalize everything you've learned here. Money skills are valuable, and learning them now will give you a stable and faster upstart in life because you're mature in money. A money-mature person is a mentally mature person.

Your teenage years are the foundational time to build strong and reliable money skills. Having a strong sense of control over your finances can help you grow in all aspects of your life. Throughout this book, we've highlighted all the money skills you need to acquire and master during these foundational years. We've talked extensively about budgeting and saving, the two most important money skills you would ever need to acquire.

Now you understand that budgeting is the process of allocating funds to a particular expense, and saving is keeping a certain amount of money aside. Financial discipline is the ability to make wise financial decisions with your money. It's similar to making a strategy for your financial expenses and savings.

Investing is not only for adults. You can invest at a young age, and there is no minimum or maximum amount required. Investing is when you use your money to invest in places and things that will bring you profit in the future. Digital money is real money. It is any monetary option that isn't cash.

Being financially disciplined means you're responsible with your money, and it positions you for a more secure future. Personal finance refers to the management of a person or a home's financial resources and decisions. It encompasses all the various skills highlighted in the previous chapter for financial independence.

Entrepreneurship is basically all about spotting cool opportunities to start something new or shake things up in existing businesses. Entrepreneurs are the ones who are bold enough to take on the adventure of launching and running businesses, all in the hope of making some cash and adding value.

Take all you've learned here and implement the methods one after the other. Start by planning to budget with the next allowance or income you receive. In that plan, try to save and reduce impulse buys. You won't get it on the first try. Even if you do, you won't always be at the top of your game. It's okay to get tired, but it's not okay to give up. I am confident that you won't give up.

Good luck!

A FREE GIFT TO OUR READERS

For being our valued reader, we are offering you 4 books absolutely FREE today.

What You'll Get:

- ✔ **11 Essential Life Skills** Every Teen Needs to Learn Before Leaving Home

- ✔ How to **Be A Calm Parent** Even When Your Teens Drive You Crazy

- ✔ 15 Tips to **Build Self-Esteem and Confidence** in Teen Boys & Girls

- ✔ **Anxiety Help** for Teenagers

Please scan the below QR code to download now.

Alternatively, you can visit:
www.thementorbucket.com/gift-mstg

MORE RECOMMENDED BOOKS

SELF-LOVE FOR TEEN GIRLS

9 Steps to Transform Your Mindset, Build Self-Esteem, and Create a Life You Truly Love

Get more details here:
www.thementorbucket.com/self-love

LIFE SKILLS FOR TEENS WORKBOOK

35+ Essentials for Winning in the Real World | How to Cook, Manage Money, Drive a Car, and Develop Manners, Social Skills, and More

Get more details here:
www.thementorbucket.com/life-skills-teens

WANT TO READ MORE?

Before I close, I recommend you to read our other books in the series. These books are written especially for teens and their parents. You'll find them very helpful.

Get more details here:
www.thementorbucket.com/resources

www.ingramcontent.com/pod-product-compliance
Lightning Source LLC
Chambersburg PA
CBHW071203120626
46546CB00006B/2401